The Scientific Background to Modern Philosophy

Selected Readings

The Scientific Background to Modern Philosophy

Selected Readings

Edited by
Michael R. Matthews

Hackett Publishing Company
Indianapolis/Cambridge

Cover and interior design by Dan Kirklin

For further information, please address

Hackett Publishing Company, Inc.
P.O. Box 44937
Indianapolis, Indiana 46204

93   92   91   90   89   1   2   3   4   5

Library of Congress Cataloging-in-Publication Data

The Scientific background to modern philosophy.

Bibliography: p.
1. Science—Philosophy.   2. Science—Methodology.
I. Matthews, Michael R.
Q175.S4232   1989   501   88–32012
ISBN 0–87220–075–2
ISBN 0–87220–074–4 (pbk.)

CONTENTS

To

Robert S. Cohen

of Boston University.
A physicist, philosopher, friend, and generous host,
who introduced me to the themes of this book.

ACKNOWLEDGMENTS

ARISTOTLE   *Physics* and *Posterior Analytics* from Jonathan Barnes (ed.), *The Complete Works of Aristotle* (2 vols.), Princeton: Princeton University Press, 1984. Copyright 1984, The Jowett Copyright Trustees. This revised translation is based upon the original W.D. Ross (1930) Oxford University Press edition.

COPERNICUS   *The Commentariolus* and Dedication for *On the Revolutions of the Heavenly Spheres* from Edward Rosen, *Three Copernican Treatises*, New York: Dover Publications, 1959 (2nd edit.)

BACON   *The New Organon* from the Fulton H. Anderson edition, Indianapolis: Bobbs-Merrill, 1960. Copyright, Macmillan Publishers, New York.

GALILEO   *The Assayer* from A.C. Danto and S. Morgenbesser (eds.), *Philosophy of Science*, New York: World Publishing Co., 1960.

Dialogues Concerning the Two Chief World Systems from Stillman Drake (trans.), Berkeley: The University of California Press, 1953. Copyright © 1932, 1953 Regents of the University of California.

Discourses Concerning the Two New Sciences from Henry Crew & Alfonso de Salvio (trans.), New York: Macmillan, 1914. Copyright Northwestern University Press.

DESCARTES   *Discourse on Method* from *The Philosophical Works of Descartes*, 2 vols., Elizabeth S. Haldane and G.R.T. Ross (trans.), Cambridge: Cambridge University Press, 1911.

The Principles of Philosophy from V.R. and R.P. Miller (trans.), Dordrecht: D. Reidel Publishing Co., 1983. Copyright © 1983, D. Reidel Publishing Company. Reproduced by permission of Kluwer Academic Publishers.

BOYLE   *About the Excellency & Grounds of the Mechanical Hypothesis* from Marie Boas Hall (ed.), *Nature & Nature's Laws*, New York: Walker & Company, 1970. Copyright Marie Boas Hall.

HUYGENS   *Treatise On Light* from *The Wave Theory of Light*, Henry Crew (ed.), New York: American Book Company, 1900.

ix

NEWTON   *Principia* from Florian Cajori (trans.), *Newton's Principia*, Berkeley: University of California Press, 1945. Copyright © 1934, 1962 Regents of the University of California.

Opticks reprinted by permission of Dover Publications from *Opticks* by Sir Isaac Newton, New York: Dover Publications, Inc., 1952.

I would like to thank the copyright holders of the above for permission to reproduce the materials.

INTRODUCTION

The development of modern philosophy in the seventeenth century is clearly linked with the development of modern science. The Scientific Revolution had philosophical ramifications. Continental rationalism was developed from and appealed to the mathematical and *a prioristic* aspects of the new science. British empiricism likewise sought justification in the observational and experimental aspects of the new science. Immanuel Kant and John Locke developed philosophical treatises that took explicit cognisance of Isaac Newton's physics. Bishop Berkeley was a critic of Newton. Thomas Hobbes visited Galileo, and his philosophical method was modeled upon the great scientist's new method in mechanics.

The history of science and the history of philosophy have been closely connected. Unfortunately the studies of these histories have not been so closely connected. With some noteworthy exceptions (e.g., Duhem, Koyré), the history of science has been studied without much attention to the important philosophical issues to which science gave rise. Likewise, students of the history of philosophy are seldom exposed to the science that was so clearly exercising the minds of the philosophers whose work they examine. This is part of a more general ahistorical attitude that distorts, specifically, Anglo-Saxon philosophy: the great philosophers are read through very contemporary eyes.

This anthology is designed to contribute a little to bridging the unfortunate and artificial gap between the history of science and the history of philosophy. It makes accessible some of the philosophically relevant science of the Scientific Revolution. It soon becomes apparent that the very distinction between scientists and philosophers is almost impossible to draw in the sixteenth and seventeenth centuries. Those whom we now call scientists and place in the history of science curriculum were at the time known as Natural Philosophers. Galileo, Newton, and others contributed to epistemology, ontology, and metaphysics, as well as to physics. His-

1

tories of philosophy standardly omit or minimise the philosophical contribution of the "scientists" of the Scientific Revolution. This again is characteristic of an ahistorical attitude: a failure to understand and examine philosophy in its own social and, particularly, intellectual contexts.

Considerations of the methodology of science—how to appraise competing scientific claims, what confidence we can have in scientific theories, how observation relates to theory, what the role of mathematics and reason is in the construction and application of theory—are clearly on the borderland of science and philosophy. Many methodological and ontological positions in science begin life as philosophy and only later are accepted as recognisably science when they become part of a successful scientific programme. These readings include some of the methodological writings of the scientists (to use modern idiom).

But methodology ought not be divorced from the actual science it was reflecting upon. Thus the readings contain small portions of astronomy and physics. An effort has been made to illustrate the pivotal roles that mathematics (geometry) and experimentation played in the development of the new science. It is notorious that the contemporary philosophical commentators on the new science had difficulty appreciating the former and that they often collapsed the latter into simple observation or experience. And of course we must not assume that the 16th- and 17th-century scientists gave accurate philosophical accounts of their own practices.

The background to the new science was the old science of Aristotle. A little of his physics, metaphysics, and methodology are included. Of course the old science against which the Scientific Revolution was launched was being practised two thousand years after Aristotle wrote. Aristotle was mediated by the medieval scholastics. Their understanding and their sources were not always accurate. It would be more historical to include here Aristotle as he was interpreted, and thus selections from the scholastics. But there were many medieval and Renaissance "Aristotelianisms". They were informed by various other traditions. The problem of selection would be difficult. On balance, my judgment is that it is best to include some of Aristotle, to give a sense of Aristotelianism, and to draw attention to the differences between Aristotle and how he was expounded in the period of the Scientific Revolution.

I have provided a very short introduction to each selection. I have tried, as they say in cricket, to play a straight bat. Interpretative arguments rage over Aristotle, Galileo, Newton, and the others. These comprise large-scale battles over just what their philosophy amounted to and local skirmishes about the meaning of particular texts. What was interpretative orthodoxy in one age becomes succeeding ages' prime example of anachronistic misreading or ideological self-serving. I have tried to let the texts speak for themselves or, more to the point, speak to students. The object is for students to read something of the original sources, to appreciate the intellectual achievements of the authors, and to begin forming their own opinions of the philosophical worth of the material. It is the task of an editor, or instructor, to assist this object, not to preempt it.

My introductory remarks are meant to situate the selection in the text from which it was taken and to indicate in neutral terms (or nearly so) the philosophical debate to which the selection contributed.

A very limited number of readings have been chosen for the bibliography. These are widely acknowledged classics of the secondary literature. Investigation of the philosophical content of science and of the interconnections between the history of science and the history of philosophy has been a growth industry in the philosophy of science. The neglect of these investigations in philosophy has been compensated for by their energetic pursual in the philosophy of science. The bibliography indicates just some of the fruits. For each author just some pertinent literature is cited. Good guides to further literature are the entries in the *Encyclopedia of Philosophy* (Macmillan) and, more important, the *Dictionary of Scientific Biography* (Scribners).

My hope is that this anthology's selections will, in the first place, generate further interest in the primary sources. The writings of Galileo, Boyle, Newton, etc., are a joy to read. At times there is some pain, but there is always intellectual gain. Once there is familiarity with the primary sources, then the secondary sources can be informative. To substitute the latter for the former is to repeat the mistake of Galileo's opponents, who read textbooks on the moon instead of looking through the telescope.

The anthology was compiled in response to a gracious invitation by Jay Hullett of Hackett Publishing Company. Initial work was

done during a relaxing and productive summer semester in the
Philosophy Department at Virginia Polytechnic and State University, Blacksburg, in 1987. Richard Burian was a cheerful host, Roger
Ariew and Joseph Pitt were helpful colleagues. The comments of
my friend Wallis Suchting have been valuable, as have those of the
prepublication reviewers. I appreciate the time and energy that
they put into the task. Particular thanks are due to Arnold Koslow
of Brooklyn College, whose detailed criticism of the penultimate
draft considerably improved the final one. The book would have
been much delayed without the encouragement and assistance of
my friend Julie House.

ARISTOTLE

Physics   Bk. II ch. 1–3 (on nature, causes,
                         mathematics and science)
                         Bk. IV, ch. 8 (impossibility of motion
                         in a void)
                         Bk. VII, ch. 1, 2, 5 (laws of motion)

Posterior Analytics   Bk. I, ch. 1, 2 (scientific knowledge)
                         Bk. I, ch. 12 (knowledge of facts and
                         explanations of facts)

Born in 384 B.C. at Stagira, Macedonia, Aristotle died in 322 B.C.
For twenty years he was a pupil of Plato at the latter's illustrious
Academy. For a brief period he was tutor to the future Alexander
the Great. In 335 B.C. he established his own school, the Lyceum
(or Peripatetic school) in Athens. For a decade this was the center
of Greek learning. He was forced to flee Athens shortly before his
death, a death that signaled the twilight of one of the brightest
intellectual periods in human history.

For the two thousand years to the beginning of the modern world
in the early seventeenth century, philosophy and science were
dominated by the rival world views and systems of Plato and his
dissident pupil Aristotle. At different times and in different areas,
first one, then the other held sway. It is common to view the intellectual flowering of the European Renaissance and its associated
Scientific Revolution as a rediscovery and triumph of Platonic
thinking over the long-entrenched Aristotelian thought patterns
and systems of medieval scholasticism. There is some truth in this
characterisation. But there are also elements of Aristotelian thinking—its empiricism, essentialism, naturalism, and teleology—that
in various ways survived the intellectual revolution of the seven-

5

teenth century and that constantly recur in modern thought. Aristotle has indeed cast a long shadow. There can be no adequate understanding of early modern philosophy and of the new science of Galileo, Newton, and others, without some comprehension of Aristotle's world view against which the new world view was forged.

Central to all of Aristotle's thought is his concept of nature. This was essentialistic and teleological. Nature was not just matter moving around as a result of random pushes and pulls (materialism), nor was it an unintelligible and imperfect shadow of some other perfect realm (Platonism). Nature was differentiated into various species and objects, all of which had their own internal and essential dynamic for change (including local motion). Their alteration was the progressive, teleological actualisation of a preexisting potential. The universe was finite, closed, hierarchically ordered, and all its constituents were fixed. Everything had its own preordained purpose.

In the appropriate circumstances, the acorn would develop through an internally generated process of natural change. Likewise, when not interfered with, heavy objects would naturally move to their natural place at the centre of the earth. Science was largely concerned with the understanding of these natural changes in the world. The contrasting violent or chance changes were of little interest to philosophers, as they did not reveal anything of the object's nature.

The following extracts from the *Physics* outline something of Aristotle's understanding of nature, of natural change, and of the kinds of causality operating in nature. Book IV, chapter 8, was much commented upon by medieval and scholastic natural philosophers. It contains his arguments against a void. These well illustrate the naturalism of Aristotle: science was to tell us about the world we live in and see about us. In this world, the actual world, there is no void, and objects come to rest if they are not constantly pushed. Experience everywhere testifies to this. In Book VII his account of motion is further developed, and his 'laws' of motion are introduced. Galileo's and Newton's constant references to idealised situations—frictionless planes and point masses moving in a void—were at sharp odds with the practical, immediate empiricism of Aristotle.

For good reason the medievals said there could be no knowledge of nature without knowledge of motion. The foundational laws of dynamics reveal metaphysical, ontological, and epistemological riches. They represent the borderland of science and philosophy.

As well as writing extensively on science and a great range of other subject matters—ethics, metaphysics, politics, astronomy, religion, etc.—Aristotle also wrote the first comprehensive treatise on scientific methodology. This was his *Posterior Analytics*. It set the agenda for two thousand years of discussion in philosophy of science. Galileo was an avid student of this treatise. The *Posterior Analytics* deals with what it is to explain something, the place of perception in natural philosophy, and whether certainty and absolute truth are attainable in science. All are still lively topics of debate.

READING

Ackrill, J.L. *Aristotle the Philosopher*. Oxford: Oxford University Press, 1981.

Barnes, J. *The Complete Works of Aristotle*. 2 vols. Princeton: Princeton University Press, 1984.

Grene, M. *A Portrait of Aristotle*. London: Faber & Faber, 1963.

Randall, J.H., Jr. *Aristotle*. New York: Columbia University Press, 1960.

Ross, W.D. *Aristotle*. London: Methuen, 1949.

Solmsen, F. *Aristotle's System of the Physical World: A Comparison with His Predecessors*. Ithaca: Cornell University Press, 1960.

PHYSICS

BOOK II

Chapter 1: 192b–193b

Of things that exist, some exist by nature, some from other causes. By nature the animals and their parts exist, and the plants and the simple bodies (earth, fire, air, water)—for we say that these and the like exist by nature.

Note: The numbers following the chapter number refer to Immanuel Bekker's edition of the Greek text (Berlin, 1931). Chapter 1 runs from page 192, column b, to page 193, column b.

All the things mentioned plainly differ from things which are *not* constituted by nature. For each of them has within itself a principle of motion and of stationariness (in respect of place, or of growth and decrease, or by way of alteration). On the other hand, a bed and a coat and anything else of that sort, *qua* receiving these designations—i.e. in so far as they are products of art—have no innate impulse to change. But in so far as they happen to be composed of stone or of earth or of a mixture of the two, they *do* have such an impulse, and just to that extent—which seems to indicate that nature is a principle or cause of being moved and of being at rest in that to which it belongs primarily, in virtue of itself and not accidentally.

I say 'not accidentally', because (for instance) a man who is a doctor might himself be a cause of health to himself. Nevertheless it is not in so far as he is a patient that he possesses the art of medicine: it merely has happened that the same man is doctor and patient—and that is why these attributes are not always found together. So it is with all other artificial products. None of them has in itself the principle of its own production. But while in some cases (for instance houses and the other products of manual labour) that principle is in something else external to the thing, in others—those which may cause a change in themselves accidentally—it lies in the things themselves (but not in virtue of what they are).

Nature then is what has been stated. Things have a nature which have a principle of this kind. Each of them is a substance; for it is a subject, and nature is always in a subject.

The term 'according to nature' is applied to all these things and also to the attributes which belong to them in virtue of what they are, for instance the property of fire to be carried upwards—which is not a nature nor has a nature but is by nature or according to nature.

What nature is, then, and the meaning of the terms 'by nature' and 'according to nature', has been stated. *That* nature exists, it would be absurd to try to prove; for it is obvious that there are many things of this kind, and to prove what is obvious by what is not is the mark of a man who is unable to distinguish what is self-evident from what is not. (This state of mind is clearly possible. A man blind from birth might reason about colours.) Presumably therefore such persons must be talking about words without any thought to correspond.

Some identify the nature or substance of a natural object with that immediate constituent of it which taken by itself is without arrangement, e.g. the wood is the nature of the bed, and the bronze the nature of the statue.

As an indication of this Antiphon points out that if you planted a bed and the rotting wood acquired the power of sending up a shoot, it would not be a bed that would come up, but *wood* which shows that the arrangement in accordance with the rules of the art is merely an accidental attribute, whereas the substance is the other, which, further, persists continuously through the process.

But if the material of each of these objects has itself the same relation to something else, say bronze (or gold) to water, bones (or wood) to earth and so on, *that* (they say) would be their nature and substance. Consequently some assert earth, others fire or air or water or some or all of these, to be the nature of the things that are. For whatever any one of them supposed to have this character—whether one thing or more than one thing—this or these he declared to be the whole of substance, all else being its affections, states, or dispositions. Every such thing they held to be eternal (for it could not pass into anything else), but other things to come into being and cease to be times without number.

This then is one account of nature, namely that it is the primary underlying matter of things which have in themselves a principle of motion or change.

Another account is that nature is the shape or form which is specified in the definition of the thing.

For the word 'nature' is applied to what is according to nature and the natural in the same way as 'art' is applied to what is artistic or a work of art. We should not say in the latter case that there is anything artistic about a thing, if it is a bed only potentially, not yet having the form of a bed; nor should we call it a work of art. The same is true of natural compounds. What is potentially flesh or bone has not yet its own nature, and does not exist by nature, until it receives the form specified in the definition, which we name in defining what flesh or bone is. Thus on the second account of nature, it would be the shape or form (not separable except in statement) of things which have in themselves a principle of motion. (The combination of the two, e.g. man, is not nature but by nature.)

The form indeed is nature rather than the matter; for a thing is more properly said to be what it is when it exists in actuality than when it exists potentially. Again man is born from man but not bed from bed. That is why people say that the shape is not the nature of a bed, but the wood is—if the bed sprouted, not a bed but wood would come up. But even if the shape *is* art,[1] then on the same principle the shape of man is his nature. For man is born from man.

Again, nature in the sense of a coming-to-be proceeds towards nature. For it is not like doctoring, which leads not to the art of doctoring but to health. Doctoring must start from the art, not lead to it. But it is not in this way that nature is related to nature. What grows *qua* growing grows from something into something. Into what then does it grow? Not into that from which it arose but into that to which it tends. The shape then is nature.

Shape and nature are used in two ways. For the privation too is in a way form. But whether in unqualified coming to be there is privation, i.e. a contrary, we must consider later.

Chapter 2: 193b–194b

We have distinguished, then, the different ways in which the term 'nature' is used.

The next point to consider is how the mathematician differs from the student of nature; for natural bodies contain surfaces and volumes, lines and points, and these are the subject-matter of mathematics.

Further, is astronomy different from natural science or a department of it? It seems absurd that the student of nature should be supposed to know the nature of sun or moon, but not to know any of their essential attributes, particularly as the writers on nature obviously do discuss their shape and whether the earth and the world are spherical or not.

Now the mathematician, though he too treats of these things, nevertheless does not treat them as the limits of a natural body; nor does he consider the attributes indicated as the attributes of such bodies. That is why he separates them; for in thought they are separable from motion, and it makes no difference, nor does any falsity result, if they are separated. The holders of the theory of Forms do the same, though they are not aware of it; for they

---

1. Reading τέχνη, with the MSS, for Ross's φύσις.

separate the objects of natural science, which are less separable than those of mathematics. This becomes plain if one tries to state in each of the two cases the definitions of the things and of their attributes. Odd and even, straight and curved, and likewise number, line, and figure, do not involve motion; not so flesh and bone and man—*these* are defined like snub nose, not like curved.

Similar evidence is supplied by the more natural of the branches of mathematics, such as optics, harmonics, and astronomy. These are in a way the converse of geometry. While geometry investigates natural lines but not *qua* natural, optics investigates mathematical lines, but *qua* natural, not *qua* mathematical.

Since two sorts of thing are called nature, the form and the matter, we must investigate its objects as we could the essence of snubness, that is neither independently of matter nor in terms of matter only. Here too indeed one might raise a difficulty. Since there are two natures, with which is the student of nature concerned? Or should he investigate the combination of the two? But if the combination of the two, then also each severally. Does it belong then to the same or to different sciences to know each severally?

If we look at the ancients, natural science would seem to be concerned with the *matter*. (It was only very slightly that Empedocles and Democritus touched on form and essence.)

But if on the other hand art imitates nature, and it is the part of the same discipline to know the form and the matter up to a point (e.g. the doctor has a knowledge of health and also of bile and phlegm, in which health is realized and the builder both of the form of the house and of the matter, namely that it is bricks and beams, and so forth): if this is so, it would be the part of natural science also to know nature in both its senses.

Again, that for the sake of which, or the end, belongs to the same department of knowledge as the means. But the nature is the end or that for the sake of which. For if a thing undergoes a continuous change toward some end, that last stage[2] is actually that for the sake of which. (That is why the poet was carried away into making an absurd statement when he said 'he has the end for the sake of which he was born'. For not every stage that is last claims to be an end, but only that which is best.)

---

2. Reading τούτο ἔσχατον.

For the arts make their material (some simply make it, others make it serviceable), and we use everything as if it was there for our sake. (We also are in a sense an end. 'That for the sake of which' may be taken in two ways, as we said in our work *On Philosophy*.) The arts, therefore, which govern the matter and have knowledge are two, namely the art which uses the product and the art which directs the production of it. That is why the using art also is in a sense directive; but it differs in that it knows the form,[3] whereas the art which is directive as being concerned with production knows the matter. For the helmsman knows and prescribes what sort of form a helm should have, the other from what wood it should be made and by means of what operations. In the products of art, however, we make the material with a view to the function, whereas in the products of nature the matter is there all along.

Again, matter is a relative thing—for different forms there is different matter.

How far then must the student of nature know the form or essence? Up to a point, perhaps, as the doctor must know sinew or the smith bronze (i.e. until he understands the purpose of each);[4] and the student of nature is concerned only with things whose forms are separable indeed, but do not exist apart from matter. Man is begotten by man and by the sun as well. The mode of existence and essence of the separable it is the business of first philosophy to define.

Chapter 3: 194b–195b

Now that we have established these distinctions, we must proceed to consider causes, their character and number. Knowledge is the object of our inquiry, and men do not think they know a thing till they have grasped the 'why' of it (which is to grasp its primary cause). So clearly we too must do this as regards both coming to be and passing away and every kind of natural change, in order that, knowing their principles, we may try to refer to these principles each of our problems.

In one way, then, that out of which a thing comes to be and which persists, is called a cause, e.g. the bronze of the statue, the silver

---

3. Omitting ἡ ἀρχιτεκτονική.
4. Reading μέχρι τον. τίνος γάρ (Jaeger).

of the bowl, and the genera of which the bronze and the silver are species.

In another way, the form or the archetype, i.e. the definition of the essence, and its genera, are called causes (e.g. of the octave the relation of 2:1, and generally number), and the parts in the definition.

Again, the primary source of the change or rest; e.g. the man who deliberated is a cause, the father is cause of the child, and generally what makes of what is made and what changes of what is changed.

Again, in the sense of end or that for the sake of which a thing is done, e.g. health is the cause of walking about. ('Why is he walking about?' We say: 'To be healthy', and, having said that, we think we have assigned the cause.) The same is true also of all the intermediate steps which are brought about through the action of something else as means towards the end, e.g. reduction of flesh, purging, drugs, or surgical instruments are means towards health. All these things are for the sake of the end, though they differ from one another in that some are activities, other instruments.

This then perhaps exhausts the number of ways in which the term 'cause' is used.

As things are called causes in many ways, it follows that there are several causes of the same thing (not merely accidentally), e.g. both the art of the sculptor and the bronze are causes of the statue. These are causes of the statue *qua* statue, not in virtue of anything else that it may be—only not in the same way, the one being the material cause, the other the cause whence the motion comes. Some things cause each other reciprocally, e.g. hard work causes fitness and *vice versa*, but again not in the same way, but the one as end, the other as the principle of motion. Further the same thing is the cause of contrary results. For that which by its presence brings about one result is sometimes blamed for bringing about the contrary by its absence. Thus we ascribe the wreck of a ship to the absence of the pilot whose presence was the cause of its safety.

All the causes now mentioned fall into four familiar divisions. The letters are the causes of syllables, the material of artificial products, fire and the like of bodies, the parts of the whole, and the premisses of the conclusion, in the sense of 'that from which'. Of these pairs the one set are causes in the sense of what underlies, e.g. the parts, the other set in the sense of essence—the whole and the combination and the form. But the seed and the doctor and the deliberator, and generally the maker, are all sources whence the change or stationariness orginates, which the others are causes in the sense of the end or the good of the rest; for that for the sake of which tends to be what is best and the end of the things that lead up to it. (Whether we call it good or apparently good makes no difference.)

Such then is the number and nature of the kinds of cause.

Now the modes of causation are many, though when brought under heads they too can be reduced in number. For things are called causes in many ways and even within the same kind one may be prior to another: e.g. the doctor and the expert are causes of health, the relation 2:1 and number of the octave, and always what is inclusive to what is particular. Another mode of causation is the accidental and its genera, e.g. in one way Polyclitus, in another a sculptor is the cause of a statue, because being Polyclitus and a sculptor are accidentally conjoined. Also the classes in which the accidental attribute is included; thus a man could be said to be the cause of a statue or, generally, a living creature. An accidental attribute too may be more or less remote, e.g. suppose that a pale man or a musical man were said to be the cause of the statue.

All causes, both proper and accidental, may be spoken of either as potential or as actual; e.g. the cause of a house being built is either a house-builder or a house-builder building.

Similar distinctions can be made in the things of which the causes are causes, e.g. of this statue or of a statue or of an image generally, of this bronze or of bronze or of material generally. So too with the accidental attributes. Again we may use a complex expression for either and say, e.g., neither 'Polyclitus' nor a 'sculptor' but 'Polyclitus, the sculptor'.

All these various uses, however, come to six in number, under each of which again the usage is twofold. It is either what is particular or a genus, or an accidental attribute or a genus of that, and these either as a complex or each by itself; and all either as actual or as potential. The difference is this much, that causes which are actually at work and particular exist and cease to exist simultaneously with their effect, e.g. this healing person with this being-healed person and that housebuilding man with the being-built house; but this is not always true of potential causes—the house and the housebuilder do not pass away simultaneously.

In investigating the cause of each thing it is always necessary to seek what is most precise (as also in other things): thus a man builds because he is a builder, and a builder builds in virtue of his art of building. This last cause then is prior; and so generally.

Further, generic effects should be assigned to generic causes, particular effects to particular causes, e.g. statue to sculptor, this statue to this sculptor; and powers are relative to possible effects, actually operating causes to things which are actually being effected.

This must suffice for our account of the number of causes and the modes of causation.

BOOK IV

Chapter 8: 214b–216b

Let us explain again that there is no void existing separately, as some maintain. If each of the simple bodies has a natural loco-motion, e.g. fire upward and earth downward and towards the middle of the universe, it is clear that the void cannot be a cause of locomotion. What, then, *will* the void be a cause of? It is thought to be a cause of movement in respect of place, and it is not a cause of this.

Again, if void is a sort of place deprived of body, when there is a void where will a body placed in it move to? It certainly cannot move into the whole of the void. The same argument applies as against those who think that place is something separate, into which things are carried; viz. how will what is placed in it move, or rest? The same argument will apply to the void as to the up and down in place, as is natural enough since those who maintain the existence of the void make it a place.

And in what way will things be present either in place or in the void? For the result does not take place when a body is placed as a whole in a place conceived of as separate and permanent; for a part of it, unless it be placed apart, will not be in a place but in the whole. Further, if separate place does not exist, neither will void.

If people say that the void must exist, as being necessary if there is to be movement, what rather turns out to be the case, if one studies the matter, is the opposite, that not a single thing can be moved if there *is* a void; for as with those who say the earth is at rest because of the uniformity, so, too, in the void things must be at rest; for there is no place to which things can move more or less than to another; since the void in so far as it is void admits no difference.

The second reason is this: all movement is either compulsory or according to nature, and if there is compulsory movement there must also be natural (for compulsory movement is contrary to nature, and movement contrary to nature is posterior to that according to nature, so that if each of the natural bodies has not a natural movement, none of the other movements can exist); but how can there be *natural* movement if there is no difference throughout the void or the infinite? For in so far as it is infinite, there will be no up or down or middle, and in so far as it is a void, up differs no whit from down; for as there is no difference in what is nothing, there is none in the void (for the void seems to be a non-existent and a privation); but natural locomotion seems to be differentiated, so that the things that exist by nature must be differentiated. Either, then, nothing has a natural locomotion, or else there is no void.

Further, in point of fact things that are thrown move though that which gave them their impulse is not touching them, either by reason of mutual replacement, as some maintain, or because the air that has been pushed pushes them with a movement quicker than the natural locomotion of the projectile wherewith it moves to its proper place. But in a void none of these things can take place, nor can anything be moved save as that which is carried is moved.

Further, no one could say why a thing once set in motion should stop anywhere; for why should it stop *here* rather than *here*? So that a thing will either be at rest or must be moved *ad infinitum*, unless something more powerful gets in its way.

Further, things are now thought to move into the void because it yields; but in a void this quality is present equally everywhere, so that things should move in all directions.

Further, the truth of what we assert is plain from the following considerations. We see the same weight or body moving faster than another for two reasons, either because there is a difference in what it moves through, as between water, air, and earth, or because, other things being equal, the moving body differs from the other owing to excess of weight or of lightness.

Now the medium causes a difference because it impedes the moving thing, most of all if it is moving in the opposite direction, but in a secondary degree even if it is at rest; and especially a medium that is not easily divided, i.e. a medium that is somewhat dense.

A, then, will move through B in time C, and through D, which is thinner, in time E (if the length of B is equal to D), in proportion to the density of the hindering body. For let B be water and D air; then by so much as air is thinner and more incorporeal than water, A will move through D faster than through B. Let the speed have the same ratio to the speed, then, that air has to water. Then if air is twice as thin, the body will traverse B in twice the time that it does D, and the time C will be twice the time E. And always, by so much as the medium is more incorporeal and less resistant and more easily divided, the faster will be the movement.

Now there is no ratio in which the void is exceeded by body, as there is no ratio of nought to a number. For if 4 exceeds 3 by 1, and 2 by more than 1, and 1 by still more than it exceeds 2, still there is no ratio by which it exceeds 0; for that which exceeds must be divisible into the excess and that which is exceeded, so that 4 will be what it exceeds 0 by and 0. For this reason, too, a line does not exceed a point—unless it is composed of points. Similarly the void can bear no ratio to the full, and therefore neither can movement through the one to movement through the other, but if a thing moves through the thinnest medium such and such a distance in such and such a time, it moves through the void with a speed beyond any ratio. For let F be void, equal to B and to D. Then if A is to traverse and move through it in a certain time, G, a time less than E, however, the void will bear this ratio to the full. But in a time equal to G, A will traverse the part H of D. And it will surely also traverse in that time any substance F which exceeds air in thinness in the ratio which the time E bears to the time G. For if the body F be as much thinner than D as E exceeds F, A, if it moves through G, will traverse it in a time inverse to the speed of the movement, i.e. in a time equal to F. If, then, there is *no* body in G, A will traverse G still more quickly. But we suppose that its traverse of G when G was void occupied the time F. So that it will traverse G in an equal time whether G be full or void. But this is impossible. It is plain, then, that if there is a time in which it will move through any part of the void, this impossible result will follow: it will be found to traverse a certain distance, whether this be full or void, in an equal time; for there will be some body which is in the same ratio to the other body as the time is to the time.

To sum the matter up, the cause of this result is obvious, viz. that between any two movements there is a ratio (for they occupy time, and there is a ratio between any two times, so long as both are finite), but there is no ratio of void to full.

These are the consequences that result from a difference in the media; the following depend upon an excess of one moving body over another. We see that bodies which have a greater impulse either of weight or of lightness, if they are alike in other respects, move faster over an equal space, and in the ratio which their magnitudes bear to each other. Therefore, they will also move through the void with this ratio of speed. But that is impossible; for why should one move faster? (In moving through *plena* it must be so; for the greater divides them faster by its force. For a moving thing cleaves the medium either by its shape, or by the impulse which the body that is carried along or is projected possesses.) Therefore all will possess equal velocity. But this is impossible.

It is evident from what has been said, then, that, if there is a void, a result follows which is very opposite of the reason for which those who believe in a void set it up. They think that if movement in respect of place is to exist, the void must exist, separated by itself; but this is the same as to say that place is separate; and this has already been stated to be impossible.

But even if we consider it on its own merits the so-called void will be found to be really vacuous. For as, if one puts a cube in water, an amount of water equal to the cube will be displaced, so too in air (but the effect is imperceptible to sense). And indeed always, in the case of any body that can be displaced, it must, if it is not compressed, be displaced in the direction in which it is its nature to be displaced—always either down, if its locomotion is downwards as in the case of earth, or up, if it is fire, or in both directions—whatever be the nature of the inserted body. Now in the void this is impossible; for it is not body; the void must have penetrated the cube to a distance equal to that which this portion of void formerly occupied in the void, just as if the water or air had not been displaced by the wooden cube, but had penetrated right through it.

But the cube also has a magnitude equal to that occupied by the void; a magnitude which, if it is also hot or cold, or heavy or light, is none the less different in essence from all its attributes, even if it is not separable from them; I mean the bulk of the wooden cube. So that even if it were separated from everything else and were neither heavy nor light, it will occupy an equal amount of void, and fill the same place, as the part of place or of the void equal to itself. How then will the body of the cube differ from the void or place that is equal to it? And if there can be two such things, why cannot there be any number coinciding?

This, then, is one absurd and impossible implication of the theory. It is also evident that the cube will have this same volume even if it is displaced, which is an attribute possessed by all other bodies also. Therefore if this differs in no respect from its place, why need we assume a place for bodies over and above the bulk of each, if their bulk be conceived of as free from attributes? It contributes nothing to the situation if there is an equal interval attached to it as well. [Further, it ought to be clear by the study of moving things what sort of thing void is. But in fact it is found nowhere in the world. For air is something, though it does not *seem* to be so—nor, for that matter, would water, if fishes were made of iron; for the discrimination of the tangible is by touch.]

It is clear, then, from these considerations that there is no separate void.

BOOK VII

Chapter 1: 241b–243a

Everything that is in motion must be moved by something. For if it has not the source of its motion in itself it is evident that it is moved by something other than itself, for there must be something else that moves it. If on the other hand it has the source of its motion in itself, let AB be taken to represent that which is in motion of itself and not in virtue of the fact that something belonging to it is in motion. Now in the first place to assume that AB, because it is in motion as a whole and is not moved by anything external to itself, is therefore moved by itself—this is just as if, supposing that KL is moving LM and is also itself in motion, we were to deny that KM is moved by anything on the ground that it is not evident which is the part that is moving it and which the part that is moved. In the second place that which is in motion without being moved by anything does not necessarily cease from its motion because something else is at rest; but a thing must be moved by something if the fact of something else having ceased from its motion causes it to be at rest. If this is accepted, everything that is in motion must be moved by something. For if AB is assumed to be in motion, it must be divisible, since everything that is in motion is divisible. Let it be divided, then at C. Now if CB is not in motion, then AB will not be in motion; for if it is, it is clear that AC would be in motion while BC is at rest, and thus AB cannot be in motion in its own right and primarily. But *ex hypothesi* AB is in motion in its own right and primarily. Therefore if CB is not in motion AB will be at rest. But we have agreed that that which is at rest if something is not in motion must be moved by something. Consequently, everything that is in motion must be moved by something; for that which is in motion will always be divisible, and if a part of it is not in motion the whole must be at rest.

Since everything that is in motion must be moved by something, let us take the case in which a thing is in locomotion and is moved by something that is itself in motion, and that again is moved by something alse that is in motion, and that by something else, and so on continually: then the series cannot go on to infinity, but there must be some first mover. For let us suppose that this is not so and take the series to be infinite. Let A then be moved by B, B by C, C by D, and so on, each member of the series being moved by that which comes next to it. Then since *ex hypothesi* the mover while causing motion is also itself in motion, the motion of the moved and the motion of the mover must proceed simultaneously (for the mover is causing motion and the moved is being moved simultaneously); so it is evident that the motions of A, B, C, and each of the other moved movers are simultaneous. Let us take the motion of each separately and let E be the motion of A, F of B, and G and H respectively the motions of C and D; for though they are all moved severally one by another, yet we may still take the motion of each as numerically one, since every motion is from something to something and is not infinite in respect of its extreme points. By a motion that is numerically one I mean a motion that proceeds from something numerically one and the same to something numerically one and the same in a period of time numerically one and the same; for a motion may be the same generically, specifically, or numerically: it is generically the same if it is of the same category, e.g. substance or quality; it is specifically the same if it proceeds

from something specifically the same to something specifically the
same, e.g. from white to black or from good to bad, which is not
of a kind specifically distinct; it is numerically the same if it proceeds
from something numerically one to something numerically one in
the same time, e.g. from a particular white to a particular black,
or from a particular place to a particular place, in a particular time;
for if the time were not one and the same, the motion would no
longer be numerically one though it would still be specifically one.
We have dealt with this question above.[1] Now let us further take
the time in which A has completed its motion, and let it be represented by K. Then since the motion of A is finite the time will
also be finite. But since the movers and the things moved are infinite, the motion EFGH, i.e. the motion is composed of all the
individual motions, must be infinite. For the motions of A, B, and
the others may be equal, or the motions of the others may be
greater; but assuming what is possible, we find that whether they
are equal or some are greater, in both cases the whole motion is
infinite. And since the motion of A and that of each of the others
are simultaneous, the whole motion must occupy the same time as
the motion of A; but the time occupied by the motion of A is finite:
consequently the motion will be infinite in a finite time, which is
impossible.

It might be thought that what we set out to prove has thus been
shown, but our argument so far does not prove it, because it does
not yet prove that anything impossible results; for in a finite time
there may be an infinite motion, though not of one thing, but of
many: and in the case that we are considering this is so; for each
thing accomplishes its own motion, and there is no impossibility in
many things being in motion simultaneously. But if (as we see to
be universally the case) that which primarily moves locally and cor-
poreally must be either in contact with or continuous with that
which is moved, the things moved and the movers must be continuous or in contact with one another, so that together they all
form a unity: whether this unity is finite or infinite makes no difference to our present argument; for in any case since the things
in motion are infinite in number the motion will be infinite, if it is
possible for the motions to be either equal to or greater than one
another; for we shall take as actual that which is possible. If, then,

---

1. See 227b3ff.

A, B, C, D form, either finite or infinite magnitude that passes through the motion EFGH in the finite time K, it follows that an infinite motion is passed through in a finite time: and whether the magnitude in question is finite or infinite this is in either case impossible. Therefore the series must come to an end, and there must be a first mover and a first moved; for the fact that this impossibility rests on an assumption is immaterial, since the case assumed is possible, and the assumption of a possible case ought not to give rise to any impossible result.

Chapter 2: 243a–245b

That which is the first mover of a thing—in the sense that it supplies not that for the sake of which but the source of the motion—is always together with that which is moved by it (by 'together' I mean that there is nothing between them). This is universally true wherever one thing is moved by another. And since there are three kinds of motion, local, qualitative, and quantitative, there must also be three kinds of mover, that which causes locomotion, that which causes alteration, and that which causes increase or decrease.

Let us begin with locomotion, for this is the primary motion. Everything that is in locomotion is moved either by itself or by something else. In the case of things that are moved by themselves it is evident that the moved and the mover are together; for they contain within themselves their first mover, so that there is nothing in between. The motion of things that are moved by something else must proceed in one of four ways; for there are four kinds of locomotion caused by something other than that which is in motion, viz. pulling, pushing, carrying, and twirling. All forms of locomotion are reducible to these. Thus pushing on is a form of pushing in which that which is causing motion away from itself follows up that which it pushes and continues to push it; pushing off occurs when the mover does not follow up the thing that it has moved; throwing when the mover causes a motion away from itself more violent than the natural locomotion of the thing moved, which continues its course so long as it is controlled by the motion imparted to it. Again, pushing apart and pushing together are forms respectively of pushing off and pulling: pushing apart is pushing off, which may be a motion either away from the pusher or away from something else, while pushing together is pulling, which may be a motion towards something else as well as towards the puller.

We may similarly classify all the varieties of these last two, e.g. packing and combing: the former is a form of pushing together, the latter a form of pushing apart. The same is true of the other processes of combination and separation (they will all be found to be forms of pushing apart or of pushing together), except such as are involved in the processes of becoming and perishing. (At the same time it is evident that combination and separation are not a different kind of motion; for they may all be apportioned to one or other of those already mentioned.) Again, inhaling is a form of pulling, exhaling a form of pushing; and the same is true of spitting and of all other motions that proceed through the body, whether excretive or assimilative, the assimilative being forms of pulling, the excretive of pushing off. All other kinds of locomotion must be similarly reduced; for they all fall under one or other of our four heads. And again, of these four, carrying and twirling are reducible to pulling and pushing. For carrying always follows one of the other three methods; for that which is carried is in motion accidentally, because it is in or upon something that is in motion, and that which carries it is in doing so being either pulled or pushed or twirled; thus carrying belongs to all the other three kinds of motion in common. And twirling is a compound of pulling and pushing; for that which is twirling a thing must be pulling one part of the thing and pushing another part, since it impels one part away from itself and another part towards itself. If, therefore, it can be shown that that which is pushing and that which is pulling are together with that which is being pushed and that which is being pulled, it will be evident that in all locomotion there is nothing between moved and mover.

But the former fact is clear even from the definitions; for pushing is motion to something else from oneself or from something else, and pulling is motion from something else to oneself or to something else, when the motion of that which is pulling is quicker than the motion that would separate from one another the two things that are continuous; for it is this that causes one thing to be pulled on along with the other. (It might indeed be thought that there is a form of pulling that arises in another way: that wood, e.g. pulls fire in a manner different from the described above. But it makes no difference whether that which pulls is in motion or is stationary when it is pulling: in the latter case it pulls to the place where it is, while in the former it pulls to the place where it was.) Now it is impossible to move anything either from oneself to something else or from something else to oneself without being in contact with it: it is evident, therefore, that in all locomotion there is nothing between moved and mover.

Nor again is there anything intermediate between that which undergoes and that which causes alteration: this can be shown by induction; for in every case we find that the respective extremities of that which causes and that which undergoes alteration are together. For our assumption is that things that are undergoing alteration are altered in virtue of their being affected in respect of their so-called affective qualities; for every body differs from another in possessing a greater or lesser number of sensible characteristics or in possessing the same sensible characteristics in a greater or lesser degree. But the alteration of that which undergoes alteration is also caused by the above-mentioned characteristics, which are affections of some underlying quality. Thus we say that a thing is altered by becoming hot or sweet or thick or dry or white; and we make these assertions alike of what is inanimate and of what is animate, and further, where animate things are in question, we make them both of the parts that have no power of sense-perception and of the senses themselves. For in a way even the senses undergo alteration, since actual perception is a motion through the body in the course of which the sense is affected in a certain way. Thus the animate is capable of every kind of alteration of which the inanimate is capable; but the inanimate is not capable of every kind of alteration of which the animate is capable, since it is not capable of alteration in respect of the senses: moreover the inanimate is unconscious of being affected, whereas the animate is conscious of it, though there is nothing to prevent the animate also being unconscious of it when the alteration does not concern the senses. Since, then, the alteration of that which undergoes alteration is caused by sensible things, in every case of such alteration it is evident that the extremities of that which causes and that which undergoes alteration are together. For the air is continuous with the one and the body with the air. Again, the colour is continuous with the light and the light with the sight. And the same is true of hearing and smelling; for the primary mover in respect to the moved is the air. Similarly, in the case of tasting, the flavour is together with the sense of taste. And it is just the same in the case of things that are inanimate and incapable of sense-perception. Thus there can be nothing between that which undergoes and that which causes alteration.

Nor, again, can there be anything between that which suffers and that which causes increase; for that which starts the increase does so by becoming attached in such a way that the whole becomes one. Again, the decrease of that which suffers decrease is caused by a part of the thing becoming detached. So both that which causes increase and that which causes decrease must be continuous; and if two things are continuous there can be nothing between them.

It is evident, therefore, that between the moved and the mover—the first and the last—in reference to the moved there is nothing intermediate.

Chapter 5: 249b–250b

Now since a mover always moves something and is in something, and extends to something (by 'is in something' I mean that it occupies a time; and by 'extends to something' I mean that it involves a certain amount of distance—for at any moment when a thing is causing motion, it also has caused motion, so that there must always be a certain amount of distance that has been traversed and a certain amount of time that has been occupied). If, then, A is the mover, B the moved, C the distance moved, and D the time, then in the same time the same force A will move ½B twice the distance C, and in ½D it will move ½B the whole distance C; for thus the rules of proportion will be observed. Again if a given force moves a given object a certain distance in a certain time and half the distance in half the time, half the motive power will move half the object the same distance in the same time. Let E represent half the motive power A and F half B: then they are similarly related, and the motive power is proportioned to the weight, so that each force will cause the same distance to be traversed in the same time.

But if E moves F a distance C in a time D, it does not necessarily follow that E can move twice F half the distance C in the same time. If, then, A moves B a distance C in a time D, it does not follow that E, being half of A, will in the time D or in any fraction of it cause B to traverse a part of C the ratio between which and the whole of C is proportionate to that between A and E—in fact it might well be that it will cause no motion at all; for it does not follow that, if a given motive power causes a certain amount of motion, half that power will cause motion either of any particular amount or in any length of time: otherwise one man might move a ship, since both the motive power of the ship-haulers and the distance that they all cause the ship to traverse are divisible into as many parts as there are men. Hence Zeno's reasoning is false when he argues that there is no part of the millet that does not make a sound; for there is no reason why any such part should not in any length of time fail to move the air that the whole bushel moves in falling. In fact it does not of itself move even such a quantity of the air as it would move if this part were by itself; for no part even exists otherwise than potentially in the whole.

If there are two movers each of which separately moves one of two weights a given distance in a given time, then the forces in combination will move the combined weights an equal distance in an equal time; for in this case the rules of proportion apply.

Then does this hold good of alteration and of increase also? Surely it does: for there is something that causes increase and something that suffers increase, and the one causes and the other suffers a certain amount of increase in a certain amount of time. Similarly with what alters and what is altered—something is altered a certain amount, or rather degree, in a certain amount of time: thus in twice as much time twice as much alteration will be completed and twice as much alteration will occupy twice as much time; and half in half the time, and in half half, or again, in the same amount of time it will be altered twice as much.

On the other hand if that which causes alteration or increase causes a certain amount of increase or alteration in a certain amount of time, it does not necessarily follow that it will do half in half the time or in half the time half: it may happen that there will be no alteration or increase at all, the case being the same as with the weight.

POSTERIOR ANALYTICS

Book I

Chapter 1: 71a–71b

All teaching and all intellectual learning come about from already existing knowledge. This is evident if we consider it in every case; for the mathematical sciences are acquired in this fashion, and so is each of the other arts. And similarly too with arguments—both deductive and inductive arguments proceed in this way; for both produce their teaching through what we are already aware of, the former getting their premisses as from men who grasp them, the latter proving the universal through the particular's being clear. (And rhetorical arguments too persuade in the same way; for they do so either through examples, which is induction, or through enthymemes, which is deduction.)

It is necessary to be already aware of things in two ways: of some things it is necessary to believe already that they are, of some one must grasp what the thing said is, and of others both—e.g. of the fact that everything is either affirmed or denied truly, one must believe that it is; of the triangle, that it signifies *this*; and of the unit both (both what it signifies and that it is). For each of these is not equally clear to us.

But you can become familiar by being familiar earlier with some things but getting knowledge of the others at the very same time— i.e. of whatever happens to be under the universal of which you have knowledge. For that every triangle has angles equal to two right angles was already known; but that there is a triangle in the semicircle here became familiar at the same time as the induction. (For in some cases learning occurs in this way, and the last term does not become familiar through the middle—in cases dealing with what are in fact particulars and not said of any underlying subject.)

Before the induction, or before getting a deduction, you should perhaps be said to understand in a way—but in another way not. For if you did not know if it is *simpliciter*, how did you know that it has two right angles *simpliciter*? But it is clear that you understand it in *this* sense—that you understand it universally—but you do not understand it *simpliciter*. (Otherwise the puzzle in the *Meno*[1] will result; for you will learn either nothing or what you know.)

For one should not argue in the way in which some people attempt to solve it: Do you or don't you know of every pair that it is even? And when you said Yes, they brought forward some pair of which you did not think that it was, nor therefore that it was even. For they solve it by denying that people know of every pair that it is even, but only of anything of which they know that it is a pair.—

1. See Plato, *Meno* 80D.

Yet they know it of that which they have the demonstration about
and which they got their premises about; and they got them not
about everything of which they know that it is a triangle or that it
is a number, but of every number and triangle *simpliciter*. For no
proposition of such a type is assumed (that *what you know to be a
number* . . . or *what you know to be rectilineal* . . .), but they are assumed as holding of every case.

But nothing, I think, prevents one from in a sense understanding
and in a sense being ignorant of what one is learning; for what is
absurd is not that you should know in some sense what you are
learning, but that you should know it in *this* sense, i.e. in the way
and sense in which you are learning it.

Chapter 2: 71b–72b

We think we understand a thing *simpliciter* (and not in the sophistic
fashion accidentally) whenever we think we are aware both that the
explanation because of which the object is is its explanation, and
that it is not possible for this to be otherwise. It is clear, then, that
to understand is something of this sort; for both those who do not
understand and those who do understand—the former think they
are themselves in such a state, and those who do understand actually
are. Hence that of which there is understanding *simpliciter* cannot
be otherwise.

Now whether there is also another type of understanding we
shall say later; but we say now that we do know through demonstration. By demonstration I mean a scientific deduction; and by
scientific I mean one in virtue of which, by having it, we understand
something.

If, then, understanding is as we posited, it is necessary for demonstrative understanding in particular to depend on things which
are true and primitive and immediate and more familiar than and
prior to and explanatory of the conclusion (for in this way the
principles will also be appropriate to what is being proved). For
there will be deduction even without these conditions, but there
will not be demonstration; for it will not produce understanding.

Now they must be true because one cannot understand what is
not the case—e.g. that the diagonal is commensurate. And they
must depend on what is primitive and non-demonstrable because
otherwise you will not understand if you do not have a demonstration of them; for to understand that of which there is a dem-

onstration non-accidentally is to have a demonstration. They must be both explanatory and more familiar and prior—explanatory because we only understand when we know the explanation; and prior, if they are explanatory, and we are already aware of them not only in the sense of grasping them but also knowing that they are.

Things are prior and more familiar in two ways; for it is not the same to be prior by nature and prior in relation to us, nor to be more familiar and more familiar to us. I call prior and more familiar in relation to us what is nearer to perception, prior and more familiar *simpliciter* what is further away. What is most universal is furthest away, and the particulars are nearest; and these are opposite to each other.

Depending on things that are primitive is depending on appropriate principles; for I call the same thing primitive and a principle. A principle of a demonstration is an immediate proposition, and an immediate proposition is one to which there is no other prior. A proposition is the one part of a contradiction,[2] one thing said of one; it is dialectical if it assumes indifferently either part, demonstrative if it determinately assumes the one that is true.[3] [A statement is either part of a contradiction.][4] A contradiction is an opposition of which of itself excludes any intermediate; and the part of a contradiction saying something *of* something is an affirmation, the one saying something *from* something is a denial.

An immediate deductive principle I call a posit if one cannot prove it but it is not necessary for anyone who is to learn anything to grasp it; and one which it is necessary for anyone who is going to learn anything whatever to grasp, I call an axiom (for there are some such things); for we are accustomed to use this name especially of such things. A posit which assumes either of the parts of a contradiction—i.e., I mean, that something is or that something is not—I call a supposition; one without this, a definition. For a definition is a posit (for the arithmetician posits that a unit is what is quantitatively indivisible) but not a supposition (for what a unit is and that a unit is are not the same).

Since one should both be convinced of and know the object by

---

2. Reading ἀντιφάσεως for the MSS ἀποφανσεως.
3. Reading ὅτι for ὅτι.
4. I excise this sentence.

having a deduction of the sort we call a demonstration, and since this is the case when *these* things on which the deduction depends are the case, it is necessary not only to be already aware of the primitives (either all or some of them) but actually to be better aware of them. For a thing always belongs better to that thing because of which it belongs—e.g. that because of which we love is better loved. Hence if we know and are convinced because of the primitives, we both know and are convinced of them better, since it is because of them that we know and are convinced of what is posterior.

It is not possible to be better convinced than one is of what one knows, of what one in fact neither knows nor is more happily disposed toward than if one in fact knew. But this will result if someone who is convinced because of a demonstration is not already aware of the primitives, for it is necessary to be better convinced of the principles (either all or some of them) than of the conclusion.

Anyone who is going to have understanding through demonstration must not only be familiar with the principles and better convinced of them than of what is being proved, but also there must be no other thing more convincing to him or more familiar among the opposites of the principles on which a deduction of the contrary error may depend—if anyone who understands *simpliciter* must be unpersuadable.

Chapter 13:78a–79b

Understanding the fact and the reason why differ, first in the same science—and in that in two ways: in one way, if the deduction does not come about through immediates (for the primitive explanation is not assumed, but understanding of the reason why occurs in virtue of the primitive explanation); in another, if it is through immediates but not through the explanation but through the more familiar of the converting terms. For nothing prevents the nonexplanatory one of the counterpredicated terms from sometimes being more familiar, so that the demonstration will occur through this.

E.g. that the planets are near, through their not twinkling: let C be the planets, B not twinkling, A being near. Thus it is true to say B of C; for the planets do not twinkle. But also to say A of B; for what does not twinkle is near (let this be got through induction or through perception). So it is necessary that A belongs to C; so that it has been demonstrated that the planets are near. Now this deduction is not of the reason why but of the fact; for it is not because they do not twinkle that they are near, but because they are near they do not twinkle.

But it is also possible for the latter to be proved through the former, and the demonstration will be of the reason why—e.g. let *C* be the planets, *B* being near, *A* not twinkling. Thus *B* belongs to *C* and *A* to *B*; so that *A* belongs to *C*. And the deduction is of the reason why; for the primitive explanation has been assumed.

Again, take the way they prove that the moon is spherical through its increases—for if what increases in this way is spherical and the moon increases, it is evident that it is spherical. Now in this way the deduction of the fact comes about; but if the middle term is posited the other way about, we get the deduction of the reason why; for it is not because of the increases that it is spherical, but because is is spherical it gets increases of this sort. Moon, *C*; spherical, *B*; increases, *A*.

But in cases in which the middle terms do not convert and the non-explanatory term is more familiar, the fact is proved but the reason why is not.

Again, in cases in which the middle is positioned outside—for in these too the demonstration is of the fact and not of the reason why; for the explanation is not mentioned. E.g. why does the wall not breathe? Because it is not an animal. For if this were explanatory of breathing—i.e. if the denial is explanatory of something's not belonging, the affirmation is explantory of its belonging (e.g. if imbalance in the hot and cold elements is explanatory of not being healthy, their balance is explanatory of being healthy), and similarly too if the affirmation is explanatory of something's belonging, the denial is of its not belonging. But when things are set out in this way what we have said does not result; for not every animal breathes. The deduction of such an explanation comes about in the middle figure. E.g. let *A* be animal, *B* breathing, *C* wall: then *A* belongs to every *B* (for everything breathing is an animal), but to no *C*, so that *B* too belongs to no *C*—therefore the wall does not breathe.

Explanations of this sort resemble those which are extravagantly stated (that consists in arguing by setting the middle term too far away)—e.g. Anacharsis, argument that there are no flute-girls among the Scyths, for there are no vines.

Thus with regard to the same science (and with regard to the position of the middle terms) there are these differences between the deduction of the fact and that of the reason why.

The reason why differs from the fact in another fashion, when each is considered by means of a different science. And such are those which are related to each other in such a way that the one is under the other, e.g. optics to geometry, and mechanics to solid geometry, and harmonics to arithmetic, and star-gazing to astronomy. Some of these sciences bear almost the same name—e.g. mathematical and nautical astronomy, and mathematical and acoustical harmonics. For here it is for the empirical scientists to know the fact and for the mathematical to know the reason why; for the latter have the demonstrations of the explanations, and often they do not know the fact, just as those who consider the universal often do not know some of the particulars through lack of observation.

These are those which, being something different in substance, make use of forms. For mathematics is about forms, for its objects are not said of any underlying subject—for even if geometrical objects are said of some underlying subject, still it is not *as* being said of an underlying subject that they are studied.

Related to optics as this is related to geometry, there is another science related to it—viz. the study of the rainbow; for it is for the natural scientist to know that fact, and for the study of optics— either *simpliciter* or mathematical—to know the reason why. And many even of those sciences which are not under one another are related like this—e.g. medicine to geometry; for it is for the doctor to know the fact that circular wounds heal more slowly, and for the geometer to know the reason why.

COPERNICUS

Nicolaus Copernicus was born in Poland of German parents in 1473, twenty years after the Turkish capture of Constantinople precipitated the migration of Eastern scholars and libraries into Europe. He studied law, medicine, theology, Greek, and Latin in Italy. There he became engaged by the rediscovered Greek learning, particularly Plato. In 1512 he began his career as a canon at Frauenburg Cathedral. In the same year he circulated the first draft, the *Commentariolus* (the *Little Commentary*), of his epochal heliocentric theory of the solar system. The final version, *Six Books Concerning the Revolutions of the Heavenly Spheres*, was published in 1543, the year of his death.

His heliocentric, rotating-earth theory of the solar system was put forward in opposition to the long established earth-centered theory proposed by Ptolemy in A.D. 150. They were both answers to the astronomical task purportedly enunciated by Plato. In the words of Simplicius,

> Plato lays down the principle that the heavenly bodies' motion is circular, uniform, and constantly regular. Thereupon he sets the mathematicians the following problem: What circular motions, uniform and perfectly regular, are to be admitted as hypotheses so that

it might be possible to save the appearances presented by the
planets?[1]

There was an accumulated mass of information concerning the
planetary appearances: times of rising and setting of planets, periodic reversals in their constant easterly paths, their changing
brightness, the relative position of planets against the stars, etc.
Plato's very question well illustrates the interconnection of philosophy, physics, and mathematics so characteristic of the astronomical and, more generally, the scientific tradition. Philosophy
dictated that there was an order to be found behind the planets'
chaotic appearances and, further, that their movements would be
constant and regular. Mathematics told philosophers that the most
perfect movements were circular. Given these constraints, the astronomers had to produce a model of regular, circular movements
that resulted in the apparent movements of the planets. Then as
today, the mind constructs a model that gives order to sense impressions.

The Aristotelian tradition, following Eudoxus, proposed a realist,
mechanistic model, whereby the planets were embedded in moving
homocentric crystalline spheres, the outermost one, moved by the
Prime Mover, relaying its movement to the inner spheres. This
satisfied religion and the need for a causal mechanism, but it only
imperfectly saved the appearances. Ptolemy launched an antirealist,
instrumentalist tradition in astronomy with his model of circular
deferents, epicycles, and eccentrics. It was a complicated model,
but it was consistent with common sense, philosophy, physics, and
the Christian religion. Ptolemy was prepared to put aside the question of the actual mechanism for planetary motion and instead to
concentrate on perfecting his epicyclic model, so as better to save
the appearances. For mathematical astronomy, how the planets actually move was of little concern, provided the model agreed with
how they appeared to move. Correct prediction of astronomical
phenomena was the overriding concern of the Ptolemaic tradition.

Copernicus shared all the classic metaphysics concerning the necessity for planetary motion to be circular and regular. He did
understand the relativity of perception—whether subjects or ob-

---

1. Quoted in Pierre Duhem, *To Save the Phenomena*, Chicago: University of Chicago
Press, 1985, p. 5.

jects move, appearances stay the same. In answering Plato's question, he simply changed the reference point of the solar system. Everything went in circles about the sun (or almost, as Copernicus actually had the sun displaced from the centre of his model in order to allow for the apparent speeding up and slowing down of the planets). Hence many have said that Copernicus ought be regarded as the last great medieval astronomer rather than the first modern one.

But if the Copernican system simplified celestial physics, it greatly complicated terrestrial physics. A spinning, revolving earth had all manner of counterintuitive and counterexperiential consequences: there should be a constant wind from the east, bodies ought to fly off the earth, dropped objects ought not to land beneath the points where they are released, etc. Copernicus did not provide a new physics to support his new astronomy: he saved celestial appearances but lost terrestrial ones. Nor did he provide a new metaphysics and epistemology, nor a new theological interpretation of the oft-quoted scriptural texts against a moving earth.

The Protestant scholar Andreas Osiander (1498–1552) inserted an unsigned preface into the *Revolutions* (this is not Copernicus's own Dedication, which follows) extolling an instrumentalist view of science and saying that its heliocentric model was in the tradition of mathematical astronomy, where truth was of little account compared to the calculatory function of the model. This deflected religious criticism, but clearly it did not represent the mind of Copernicus. He thought that his system was the actual system of the world: it was truth, not an algorithm.

Within one hundred and fifty years, the efforts of Kepler, Galileo, Newton, and others would sweep away the old circles and, to varying degrees, the old philosophy and theology and would provide a new physics of inertial motion and force. All of this constituted the Copernican Revolution, a revolutionary movement in which science and philosophy were inseparable.

READING

Rosen, Edward, ed. *Three Copernican Treatises*. second edition. New York: Dover, 1959. Contains *The Little Commentary*.

Great Books of the Westen World, vol. 16. Chicago: Encyclopedia Britannica, 1952. Contains *On the Revolutions of the Heavenly Spheres.*

Armitage, Angus. *The World of Copernicus.* New York: Mentor, 1951.

Kuhn, Thomas S. *The Copernican Revolution.* New York: Random House, 1957.

THE COMMENTARIOLUS

Nicholas Copernicus
Sketch of His Hypotheses
for the
Heavenly Motions

Our ancestors assumed, I observe, a large number of celestial spheres for this reason especially, to explain the apparent motion of the planets by the principle of regularity. For they thought it altogether absurd that a heavenly body, which is a perfect sphere, should not always move uniformly. They saw that by connecting and combining regular motions in various ways they could make any body appear to move to any position.

Callippus and Eudoxus, who endeavored to solve the problem by the use of concentric spheres, were unable to account for all the planetary movements; they had to explain not merely the apparent revolutions of the planets but also the fact that these bodies appear to us sometimes to mount higher in the heavens, sometimes to descend; and this fact is incompatible with the principle of concentricity. Therefore it seemed better to employ eccentrics and epicycles, a system which most scholars finally accepted.

Yet the planetary theories of Ptolemy and most other astronomers, although consistent with the numerical data, seemed likewise to present no small difficulty. For these theories were not adequate unless certain equants were also conceived; it then appeared that a planet moved with uniform velocity neither on its deferent nor about the center of its epicycle. Hence a system of this sort seemed neither sufficiently absolute nor sufficiently pleasing to the mind.

Having become aware of these defects, I often considered

whether there could perhaps be found a more reasonable arrangement of circles, from which every apparent inequality would be
derived and in which everything would move uniformly about its
proper center, as the rule of absolute motion requires. After I had
addressed myself to this very difficult and almost insoluble problem,
the suggestion at length came to me how it could be solved with
fewer and much simpler constructions than were formerly used, if
some assumptions (which are called axioms) were granted me. They
follow in this order.

Assumptions

1. There is no one center of all the celestial circles or spheres.
2. The center of the earth is not the center of the universe, but
   only of gravity and of the lunar sphere.
3. All the spheres revolve about the sun as their mid-point, and
   therefore the sun is the center of the universe.
4. The ratio of the earth's distance from the sun to the height of
   the firmament is so much smaller than the ratio of the earth's
   radius to its distance from the sun that the distance from the
   earth to the sun is imperceptible in comparison with the height
   of the firmament.
5. Whatever motion appears in the firmament arises not from
   any motion of the firmament, but from the earth's motion. The
   earth together with its circumjacent elements performs a complete rotation on its fixed poles in a daily motion, while the
   firmament and highest heaven abide unchanged.
6. What appear to us as motions of the sun arise not from its
   motion but from the motion of the earth and our sphere, with
   which we revolve about the sun like any other planet. The earth
   has, then, more than one motion.
7. The apparent retrograde and direct motion of the planets
   arises not from their motion but from the earth's. The motion
   of the earth alone, therefore, suffices to explain so many apparent inequalities in the heavens.

Having set forth these assumptions, I shall endeavor briefly to
show how uniformity of the motions can be saved in a systematic
way. However, I have thought it well, for the sake of brevity, to

omit from this sketch mathematical demonstrations, reserving these
for my larger work. But in the explanation of the circles I shall set
down here the lengths of the radii; and from these the reader who
is not unacquainted with mathematics will readily perceive how
closely this arrangement of circles agrees with the numerical data
and observations.

Accordingly, let no one suppose that I have gratuitously asserted,
with the Pythagoreans, the motion of the earth; strong proof will
be found in my exposition of the circles. For the principal arguments by which the natural philosophers attempt to establish the
immobility of the earth rest for the most part on the appearances;
it is particularly such arguments that collapse here, since I treat
the earth's immobility as due to an appearance.

The Order of the Spheres

The celestial spheres are arranged in the following order. The
highest is the immovable sphere of the fixed stars, which contains
and gives position to all things. Beneath it is Saturn, which Jupiter
follows, then Mars. Below Mars is the sphere on which we revolve;
then Venus; last is Mercury. The lunar sphere revolves about the
center of the earth and moves with the earth like an epicycle. In
the same order also, one planet surpasses another in speed of revolution, according as they trace greater or smaller circles. Thus Saturn completes its revolution in thirty years, Jupiter in twelve, Mars
in two and one-half, and the earth in one year; Venus in nine
months, Mercury in three.

The Apparent Motions of the Sun

The earth has three motions. First, it revolves annually in a great
circle about the sun in the order of the signs, always describing
equal arcs in equal times; the distance from the center of the circle
to the center of the sun is $\frac{1}{25}$ of the radius of the circle. The radius
is assumed to have a length imperceptible in comparison with the
height of the firmament; consequently the sun appears to revolve
with this motion, as if the earth lay in the center of the universe.
However, this appearance is caused by the motion not of the sun
but of the earth, so that, for example, when the earth is in the sign
of Capricornus, the sun is seen diametrically opposite in Cancer,
and so on. On account of the previously mentioned distance of the

sun from the center of the circle, this apparent motion of the sun is not uniform, the maximum inequality being 2⅙°. The line drawn from the sun through the center of the circle is invariably directed toward a point of the firmament about 10° west of the more brilliant of the two bright stars in the head of Gemini, therefore when the earth is opposite this point, and the center of the circle lies between them, the sun is seen at is greatest distance from the earth. In this circle, then, the earth revolves together with whatever else is included within the lunar sphere.

The second motion, which is peculiar to the earth, is the daily rotation on the poles in the order of the signs, that is, from west to east. On account of this rotation the entire universe appears to revolve with enormous speed. Thus does the earth rotate together with its circumjacent waters and encircling atmosphere.

The third is the motion in declination. For the axis of the daily rotation is not parallel to the axis of the great circle, but is inclined to it at an angle that intercepts a portion of a circumference, in our time about 23½°. Therefore, while the center of the earth always remains in the plane of the ecliptic, that is, in the circumference of the great circle, the poles of the earth rotate, both of them describing small circles about centers equidistant from the axis of the great circle. The period of this motion is not quite a year and is nearly equal to the annual revolution on the great circle. But the axis of the great circle is invariably directed toward the points of the firmament which are called the poles of the ecliptic. In like manner the motion in declination, combined with the annual motion in their joint effect upon the poles of the daily rotation, would keep these poles constantly fixed at the same points of the heavens, if the periods of both motions were exactly equal. Now with the long passage of time is has become clear that this inclination of the earth to the firmament changes. Hence it is the common opinion that the firmament has several motions in conformity with a law not yet sufficiently understood. But the motion of the earth can explain all these changes in a less surprising way. I am not concerned to state what the path of the poles is. I am aware that, in lesser matters, a magnetized iron needle always points in the same direction. It has nevertheless seemed a better view to ascribe the changes to a sphere, whose motion governs the movements of the poles. This sphere must doubtless be sublunar.

DEDICATION OF THE REVOLUTIONS OF THE HEAVENLY SPHERES

By Nicolaus Copernicus (1543)
To Pope Paul III

I can easily conceive, most Holy Father, that as soon as some people learn that in this book which I have written concerning the revolutions of the heavenly bodies, I ascribe certain motions to the Earth, they will cry out at once that I and my theory should be rejected. For I am not so much in love with my conclusions as not to weigh what others will think about them, and although I know that the meditations of a philosopher are far removed from the judgment of the laity, because his endeavor is to seek out the truth in all things, so far as this is permitted by God to the human reason, I still believe that one must avoid theories altogether foreign to orthodoxy. Accordingly, when I considered in my own mind how absurd a performance it must seem to those who know that the judgment of many centuries has approved the view that the Earth remains fixed as center in the midst of the heavens, if I should, on the contrary, assert that the Earth moves; I was for a long time at a loss to know whether I should publish the commentaries which I have written in proof of its motions, or whether it were not better to follow the example of the Pythagoreans and of some others, who were accustomed to transmit the secrets of Philosophy not in writing but orally, and only to their relatives and friends, as the letter from Lysis to Hipparchus bears witness. They did this, it seems to me, not as some think, because of a certain selfish reluctance to give their views to the world, but in order that the noblest truths, worked out by the careful study of great men, should not be despised by those who are vexed at the idea of taking great pains with any forms of literature except such as would be profitable, or by those who, if they are driven to the study of Philosophy for its own sake by the admonitions and the example of others, nevertheless, on account of their stupidity, hold a place among philosophers similar to that of drones among bees. Therefore, when I considered this carefully, the contempt which I had to fear because of the novelty and apparent absurdity of my view, nearly induced me to abandon utterly the work I had begun.

My friends, however, in spite of long delay and even resistance on my part, withheld me from this decision. First among these was Nicolaus Schonberg, Cardinal of Capua, distinguished in all branches of learning. Next to him comes my very dear friend, Tidemann Giese, Bishop of Culm, a most earnest student, as he is, of sacred and, indeed, of all good learning. The latter has often urged me, at times even spurring me on with reproaches, to publish and at last bring to the light the book which had lain in my study not nine years merely, but already going on four times nine. Not a few other very eminent and scholarly men made the same request, urging that I should no longer through fear refuse to give out my work for the common benefit of students of Mathematics. They said I should find that the more absurd most men now thought this theory of mine concerning the motion of the Earth, the more admiration and gratitude it would command after they saw in the publication of my commentaries the mist of absurdity cleared away by most transparent proofs. So, influenced by these advisors and this hope, I have at length allowed my friends to publish the work, as they had long besought me to do.

But perhaps Your Holiness will not so much wonder that I have ventured to publish these studies of mine, after having taken such pains in elaborating them that I have not hesitated to commit to writing my views of the motion of the Earth, as you will be curious to hear how it occurred to me to venture, contrary to the accepted view of mathematicians, and well-nigh contrary to common sense, to form a conception of any terrestrial motion whatsoever. Therefore I would not have it unknown to your Holiness, that the only thing which induced me to look for another way of reckoning the movements of the heavenly bodies was that I knew that mathematicians by no means agree in their investigations thereof. For, in the first place, they are so much in doubt concerning the motion of the sun and the moon, that they can not even demonstrate and prove by observation the constant length of a complete year; and in the second place, in determining the motions both of these and of the five other planets, they fail to employ consistently one set of first principles and hypotheses, but use methods of proof based only upon the apparent revolutions and motions. For some employ concentric circles only; others, eccentric circles and epicycles; and even by these means they do not completely attain the desired end. For, although those who have depended upon concentric circles have shown that certain diverse motions can be deduced from these, yet they have not succeeded thereby in laying down any sure principle, corresponding indisputably to the phenomena. These, on the other hand, who have devised systems of eccentric circles, although they seem in great part to have solved the apparent movements by calculations which by these eccentrics are made to fit, have nevertheless introduced many things which seem to contradict the first principles of the uniformity of motion. Nor have they been able to discover or calculate from these the main point, which is the shape of the world and the fixed symmetry of its parts; but their procedure has been as if someone were to collect hands, feet, a head, and other members from various places, all very fine in themselves, but not proportionate to one body, and no single one corresponding in its turn to the others, so that a monster rather than a man would be formed from them. Thus in their process of demonstration which they term a "method," they are found to have omitted something essential, or to have included something foreign and not pertaining to the matter in hand. This certainly would never have happened to them if they had followed fixed principles; for if the hypotheses they assumed were not false, all that resulted therefrom would be verified indubitably. Those things which I am saying now may be obscure, yet they will be made clearer in their proper place.

Therefore, having turned over in my mind for a long time this uncertainty of the traditional mathematical methods of calculating the motions of the celestial bodies, I began to grow disgusted that no more consistent scheme of the movements of the mechanism of the universe, set up for our benefit by that best and most law abiding Architect of all things, was agreed upon by philosophers who otherwise investigate so carefully the most minute details of this world. Wherefore I undertook the task of rereading the books of all the philosophers I could get access to, to see whether any one ever was of the opinion that the motions of the celestial bodies were other than those postulated by the men who taught mathematics in the schools. And I found first, indeed, in Cicero, that Niceta perceived that the Earth moved; and afterward in Plutarch I found that some others were of this opinion, whose words I have seen fit to quote here, that they may be accessible to all:—

"Some maintain that the Earth is stationary, but Philolaus the Pythagorean says that it revolves in a circle about the fire of the ecliptic, like the sun and moon. Heraklides of Pontus and Ekphantus the Pythagorean made the Earth move, not changing its position, however, confined in its falling and rising around its own center in the manner of a wheel."

Taking this as a starting point, I began to consider the mobility of the Earth; and although the idea seemed absurd, yet because I knew that the liberty had been granted to others before me to postulate all sorts of little circles for explaining the phenomena of the stars, I thought I also might easily be permitted to try whether by postulating some motion of the Earth, more reliable conclusions could be reached regarding the revolution of the heavenly bodies, than those of my predecessors.

And so, after postulating movements, which, farther on in the book, I ascribe to the Earth, I have found by many and long observations that if the movements of the other planets are assumed for the circular motion of the Earth and are substituted for the revolution of each star, not only do their phenomena follow logically therefrom, but the relative positions and magnitudes both of the stars and all their orbits, and of the heavens themselves, become so closely related that in none of its parts can anything be changed without causing confusion in the other parts and in the whole universe. Therefore, in the course of the work I have followed this plan: I describe in the first book all the positions of the orbits together with the movements which I ascribe to the Earth, in order that this book might contain, as it were, the general scheme of the universe. Thereafter in the remaining books, I set forth the motions of the other stars and of all their orbits together with the movement of the Earth, in order that one may see from this to what extent the movements and appearances of the other stars and their orbits can be saved, if they are transferred to the movement of the Earth. Nor do I doubt that ingenious and learned mathematicians will sustain me, if they are willing to recognize and weigh, not superficially, but with that thoroughness which Philosophy demands above all things, those matters which have been adduced by me in this work to demonstrate these theories. In order, however, that both the learned and the unlearned equally may see that I do not avoid anyone's judgment, I have preferred to dedicate these lucubrations of mine to Your Holiness rather than to any other, because, even in this remote corner of the world where I live, you are considered to be the most eminent man in dignity of rank and in love of all learning and even of mathematics, so that by your authority and judgment you can easily suppress the bites of slanderers, albeit the proverb hath it that there is no remedy for the bite of a sycophant. If perchance there shall be idle talkers, who, though they are ignorant of all mathematical sciences, nevertheless assume the right to pass judgment on these things, and if they should dare to criticise and attack this theory of mine because of some passage of Scripture which they have falsely distorted for their own purpose, I care not at all; I will even despise their judgment as foolish. For it is not unknown that Lactantius, otherwise a famous writer but a poor mathematician, speaks most childishly of the shape of the Earth when he makes fun of those who said that the Earth has the form of a sphere. It should not seem strange then to zealous students, if some such people shall ridicule us also. Mathematics are written for mathematicians, to whom, if my opinion does not deceive me, our labors will seem to contribute something to the ecclesiastical state whose chief office Your Holiness now occupies; for when not so very long ago, under Leo X, in the Lateran Council the question of revising the ecclesiastical calendar was discussed, it then remained unsettled, simply because the length of the years and months, and the motions of the sun and moon were held to have been not yet sufficiently determined. Since that time, I have given my attention to observing these more accurately, urged on by a very distinguished man, Paul, Bishop of Fossombrone, who at that time had charge of the matter. But what I may have accomplished herein I leave to the judgment of Your Holiness in particular, and to that of all other learned mathematicians; and lest I seem to Your Holiness to promise more regarding the usefulness of the work than I can perform, I now pass to the work itself.

BACON

The New Organon (1620)	Aphorisms 31–46 (method of the new science, idols of the mind) Aphorisms 95–96 (perception, reason and experiment in science)

Francis Bacon was the major English philosopher of the Renaissance period. He was born in 1561; he entered Cambridge University at twelve years of age; after studying Plato, Aristotle, and the scholastics, he graduated at fifteen years of age; a year later, he was an assistant ambassador to France; at twenty-five years of age, he commenced a thirty-six-year career in the English Parliament, which culminated in his being made Lord Chancellor in 1618; then followed a serious bribery case against him, which resulted in his civil offices being stripped from him; he died in 1626. His first major philosophical work, *The Advancement of Learning,* was published in 1605; his second and best known, the *Novum Organum,* was published in 1620. His death came eighty years after that of Luther and Copernicus; it occurred whilst Galileo, Kepler, Harvey, Descartes, and others were forging the new science.

How well Bacon understood the Scientific Revolution that he championed has been much debated. He clearly did not appreciate the powerful role that the newly introduced mathematical techniques had in science. He dismissed Copernicus as a 'man who did not care what fictions he introduced into nature, provided his calculations answer.' One can only conjecture what he would have made of Galileo's mature physics, with its many imaginary experiments, geometrically argued conclusions, and mathematical representations which, as the Aristotelians recognised, did violence to the facts.

Although Bacon contributed little to the new science, he was

45

greatly esteemed by the succeeding generation of scientists and natural philosophers. Robert Hooke in his *Micrographia* (1665) referred to him as the 'thrice-blessed Verulam.' (Bacon had been made Lord Verulam in 1618.) The founding members of the Royal Society eulogised him. A century and a half later, Immanuel Kant dedicated his most un-Baconlike *Critique of Pure Reason* (1781) to him.

Bacon thought that Aristotelianism could not be reformed: rather one had to begin anew the quest for knowledge. His 'New Method' was inductivism. He is regarded as the father of British Empiricism. His epistemology was developed on the assumption that there is an external world that a perceiving subject confronts and gains knowledge of through sense impressions. The less the subject contributes, the more truthfully nature can speak. In the preface to *The Great Instauration* (a brief promissory note detailing his division of the sciences) he opines that success in science 'all depends on keeping the eye steadily fixed upon the facts of nature and so receiving their images simply as they are.' This idea of the 'immaculate perception' became a leading motif of empiricism. Two centuries later, John Stuart Mill repeats it when he speaks of entry to the Kingdom of Knowledge being like entry to the Kingdom of Heaven—one has to become as unprejudiced as little children.

Bacon is highly regarded for detailing the causes of faulty cognition. His brief aphorisms on the 'Idols of the Mind' are harbingers of modern studies in linguistics, social psychology, perception, and ideology. We recognise clearly how language, class, race, sex, human interests all affect perception and judgement. Bacon was also aware that theoretical frameworks determine what and how things are seen. His response became the hallmark of empiricism: try to find theory-free observational foundations upon which to inductively create a secure science.

Auguste Comte and Ernst Mach developed this positivist programme in the nineteenth century; it was further developed by the Vienna Circle and Logical Positivists in the twentieth.[1] The relevance of empiricism to scientific practice and justification is no longer as obvious as it once seemed.[2]

---

1. A.J. Ayer, ed. *Logical Positivism*. New York: Macmillan, 1959.
2. A good account of this much-debated issue is given in the Introduction to Fred-

READING

Dick, Hugh C. *Selected Writings of Francis Bacon*. New York: Random House, 1955.

Farrington, Benjamin. *Francis Bacon, Philosopher of Industrial Science*. London: Lawrence & Wishart, 1951.

Horton, Mary. "In Defense of Francis Bacon," *Studies in the History and Philosophy of Science*. 1973, 4(3): 241–278.

Quinton, Anthony. *Francis Bacon*. Oxford: Oxford University Press, 1980.

Vickers, Brian. *Essential Articles for the Study of Francis Bacon*. Connecticut, London: Sidgwick & Johnson, 1968.

THE NEW ORGANON

APHORISMS 31–46

XXXI

It is idle to expect any great advancement in science from the superinducing and engrafting of new things upon old. We must begin anew from the very foundations, unless we would revolve forever in a circle with mean and contemptible progress.

XXXII

The honor of the ancient authors, and indeed of all, remains untouched, since the comparison I challenge is not of wits or faculties, but of ways and methods, and the part I take upon myself is not that of a judge, but of a guide.

XXXIII

This must be plainly avowed: no judgment can be rightly formed either of my method or of the discoveries to which it leads, by means of anticipations (that is to say, of the reasoning which is now in

---

erick Suppe, *The Structure of Scientific Theories*, Urbana: University of Illinois Press, 1977.

use); since I cannot be called on to abide by the sentence of a tribunal which is itself on trial.

XXXIV

Even to deliver and explain what I bring forward is no easy matter, for things in themselves new will yet be apprehended with reference to what is old.

XXXV

It was said by Borgia of the expedition of the French into Italy, that they came with chalk in their hands to mark out their lodgings, not with arms to force their way in. I in like manner would have my doctrine enter quietly into the minds that are fit and capable of receiving it; for confutations cannot be employed when the difference is upon first principles and very notions, and even upon forms of demonstration.

XXXVI

One method of delivery alone remains to us which is simply this: we must lead men to the particulars themselves, and their series and order; while men on their side must force themselves for a while to lay their notions by and begin to familiarize themselves with facts.

XXXVII

The doctrine of those who have denied that certainty could be attained at all has some agreement with my way of proceeding at the first setting out; but they end in being infinitely separated and opposed. For the holders of that doctrine assert simply that nothing can be known. I also assert that not much can be known in nature by the way which is now in use. But then they go on to destroy the authority of the senses and understanding; whereas I proceed to devise and supply helps for the same.

XXXVIII

The idols and false notions which are now in possession of the human understanding, and have taken deep root therein, not only so beset men's minds that truth can hardly find entrance, but even after entrance is obtained, they will again in the very instauration of the sciences meet and trouble us, unless men being forewarned of the danger fortify themselves as far as may be against their assaults.

XXXIX

There are four classes of Idols which beset men's minds. To these for distinction's sake I have assigned names, calling the first class *Idols of the Tribe*; the second, *Idols of the Cave*; the third, *Idols of the Market Place*; the fourth, *Idols of the Theater*.

XL

The formation of ideas and axioms by true induction is no doubt the proper remedy to be applied for the keeping off and clearing away of idols. To point them out, however, is of great use; for the doctrine of Idols is to the interpretation of nature what the doctrine of the refutation of sophisms is to common logic.

XLI

The Idols of the Tribe have their foundation in human nature itself, and in the tribe or race of men. For it is a false assertion that the sense of man is the measure of things. On the contrary, all perceptions as well of the sense as of the mind are according to the measure of the individual and not according to the measure of the universe. And the human understanding is like a false mirror, which, receiving rays irregularly, distorts and discolors the nature of things by mingling its own nature with it.

XLII

The Idols of the Cave are the idols of the individual man. For everyone (besides the errors common to human nature in general) has a cave or den of his own, which refracts and discolors the light of nature, owing either to his own proper and peculiar nature; or to his education and conversation with others; or to the reading of books, and the authority of those whom he esteems and admires; or to the differences of impressions, accordingly as they take place in a mind preoccupied and predisposed or in a mind indifferent and settled; or the like. So that the spirit of man (according as it is meted out to different individuals) is in fact a thing variable and full of perturbation, and governed as it were by chance. Whence it was well observed by Heraclitus that men look for sciences in their own lessor worlds, and not in the greater or common world.

XLIII

There are also Idols formed by the intercourse and association of men with each other, which I call Idols of the Market Place, on account of the commerce and consort of men there. For it is by discourse that men associate, and words are imposed according to the apprehension of the vulgar. And therefore the ill and unfit choice of words wonderfully obstructs the understanding. Nor do the definitions or explanations wherewith in some things learned men are wont to guard and defend themselves, by any means set the matter right. But words plainly force and overrule the understanding, and throw all into confusion, and lead men away into numberless empty controversies and idle fancies.

XLIV

Lastly, there are Idols which have immigrated into men's minds from the various dogmas of philosophies, and also from wrong laws of demonstration. These I call Idols of the Theater, because in my judgment all the received systems are but so many stage plays, representing worlds of their own creation after an unreal and scenic fashion. Nor is it only of the systems now in vogue, or only of the ancient sects and philosophies, that I speak; for many more plays of the same kind may yet be composed and in like artificial manner set forth; seeing that errors the most widely different have nevertheless causes for the most part alike. Neither again do I mean this only of entire systems, but also of many principles and axioms in science, which by tradition, credulity, and negligence have come to be received.

But of these several kinds of Idols I must speak more largely and exactly, that the understanding may be duly cautioned.

XLV

The human understanding is of its own nature prone to suppose the existence of more order and regularity in the world than it finds. And though there be many things in nature which are singular and unmatched, yet it devises for them parallels and conjugates and relatives which do not exist. Hence the fiction that all celestial bodies move in perfect circles; spirals and dragons being (except in name) utterly rejected. Hence too the element of fire with its orb is brought in, to make up the square with the other three which the sense perceives. Hence also the ratio of density of the so-called elements is arbitrarily fixed at ten to one. And so on of other dreams. And these fancies affect not dogmas only, but simple notions also.

XLVI

The human understanding when it has once adopted an opinion (either as being the received opinion or as being agreeable to itself) draws all things else to support and agree with it. And though there be a greater number and weight of instances to be found on the other side, yet these it either neglects and despises, or else by some distinction sets aside and rejects; in order that by this great and pernicious predetermination the authority of its former conclusions may remain inviolate. And therefore it was a good answer that was made by one who when they showed him hanging in a temple a picture of those who had paid their vows as having escaped shipwreck, and would have him say whether he did not now acknowledge the power of the gods,—"Aye," asked he again, "but where are they painted that were drowned after their vows?" And such is the way of all superstition, whether in astrology, dreams, omens, divine judgments, or the like; wherein men, having a delight in such vanities, mark the events where they are fulfilled, but where they fail, though this happen much oftener, neglect and pass them by. But with far more subtlety does this mischief insinuate itself into philosophy and the sciences; in which the first conclusion colors and brings into conformity with itself all that come after, though far sounder and better. Besides, independently of that delight and vanity which I have described, it is the peculiar and perpetual error of the human intellect to be more moved and excited by affirmatives than by negatives; whereas it ought properly to hold itself indifferently disposed towards both alike. Indeed in the establishment of any true axiom, the negative instance is the more forcible of the two.

APHORISMS 95–96

XCV

Those who have handled sciences have been either men of experiment or men of dogmas. The men of experiment are like the ant, they only collect and use; the reasoners resemble spiders, who make cobwebs out of their own substance. But the bee takes a middle course: it gathers its material from the flowers of the garden and of the field, but transforms and digests it by a power of its own. Not unlike this is the true business of philosophy; for it neither relies solely or chiefly on the powers of the mind, nor does it take the matter which it gathers from natural history and mechanical experiments and lay it up in the memory whole, as it finds it, but lays it up in the understanding altered and digested. Therefore from a closer and purer league between these two faculties, the experimental and the rational (such as has never yet been made), much may be hoped.

XCVI

We have as yet no natural philosophy that is pure; all is tainted and corrupted: in Aristotle's school by logic; in Plato's by natural theology; in the second school of Platonists, such as Proclus and others, by mathematics, which ought only to give definiteness to natural philosophy, not to generate or give it birth. From a natural philosophy pure and unmixed, better things are to be expected.

GALILEO

The Assayer (1623)	(on primary and secondary qualities)
Dialogues Concerning the Two chief World Systems (1632)	The Second Day, pp. 1–10 (on method and authority in science)
	The Second Day, pp. 51–55 (relativity of perception)
	The Second Day, pp. 138–40, 164–66 (the tower argument)
Discourses Concerning the Two New Sciences (1638)	The Third Day, pp. 202–208 (naturally accelerated motion, idealization, mathematics and experiment)

Galileo Galilei was born at Pisa in 1564. He died in Florence in 1642, the year of Newton's birth. He was a contemporary of most of the great figures of the Scientific Revolution—Kepler, Brahe, Bacon, Gilbert, Hobbes, Descartes, Harvey—and of John Donne and William Shakespeare. His preeminence in the history of science is assured. Immanuel Kant said of Galileo that with him 'a light broke upon all students of nature.' Newton earlier had referred to Galileo as one of 'the giants' upon whose shoulders he stood. But Galileo was a 'natural philosopher,' not just a scientist. His physics and astronomy contain developed methodological, epistemological, and ontological arguments. His contribution to philosophy deserves far more than the brief mention, if any, he is given in standard histories of philosophy.

His intellectual life divides easily into three periods: from 1588 to 1592 at the University of Pisa, where he was a teacher of mathematics; from 1592 to 1610 at the University of Padua, where he taught mathematics and physics; from 1610 to 1642 at Florence, where he was 'Chief Mathematician and Philosopher' in the court of the Grand Duke of Tuscany. At Pisa he was a well-versed teacher of Aristotelian philosophy and an enthusiast for the recently translated mathematical and physical work of the 'superhuman' Archimedes, whose name Galileo never mentions 'without a feeling of awe.' He wrote a transitional medieval/modern treatise on motion (*De Motu* 1590) which utilized Euclidean and Archimedean mathematics in the description and analysis of such physical situations as flotation, balances, and projectile motion. But the shadow of Aristotle was cast heavily over the pages—for instance, Galileo kept the distinction of natural and violent motions. When dealing with free fall, he defined acceleration as the rate of change of speed with respect to *distance*. This is a very natural, intuitive, obvious, and immediate conceptualisation. We see speed changing with distance. But this definition inhibits scientific development. It is only years later that Galileo defines acceleration in the modern terms of rate of change of speed with respect to *time*. This relatively simple point was a difficult achievement in the history of physics.

For eighteen years at the University of Padua he laid the foundations of his new science of physics. He developed the notions of the relativity of perception, circular inertia, the correct law of free fall, the parabolic analysis of projectile motion. Above all he made his physics thoroughly mathematical, and consequently he dealt with more and more abstract and ideal circumstances—perfect spheres rolling on frictionless surfaces where there was no air resistance. The Aristotelians said he was an increasingly brilliant mathematician and correspondingly poorer physicist—he was not describing and dealing with the world as it was given in experience. Inasmuch as philosophy is concerned with the type of world we know and with how we know that world, these developments in Galilean physics had philosophical consequences. They challenged Aristotelian naturalism (science tells us about a natural, undisturbed world), empiricism (knowledge of the world is gained through the senses), ontology (the planets and the earth were different substances), methodology (physics and mathematics had different methods).

The Paduan period finished with Galileo's construction of the telescope and his first observations of the moon and of the moons of Jupiter. He became a convert to Copernican astronomy. His first astronomical work was the *Starry Messenger* of 1610. He realised that the successful defence of the Copernican hypothesis required a new physics and an altered philosophy and theology. He already had the first; he began work on the latter two.

In 1615 Galileo was warned by the church not to defend the Copernican hypothesis. His great *Dialogues Concerning the Two Chief World Systems* (1632) presents the case for Copernicus in a most thinly disguised manner: so thinly disguised that he had to appear before the Inquisition the following year. After some years of house arrest, he published his other great work, *Discourses Concerning the Two New Sciences* (1638).

Galileo's work initiated much argument among astronomers, physicists, theologians, and philosophers. He forged a new abstract, mathematical physics; he developed a near-modern understanding of the role of experiment in science; he furthered understanding of causality, perception, ontology, and epistemology. *The Assayer* (1623) advanced debate in the philosophy of science, or scientific methodology. Within a few decades of his death, the Scientific (and philosophical) Revolution would triumph. Galileo's work was heterogeneous enough for both empiricists and Platonic rationalists to claim him as their champion. Understandably he was a transitional figure: two thousand years of Aristotelian philosophy and science, apparently so compatible with commonsense, everyday experience and social structures, could not be surmounted by a single figure, no matter how great a giant.

READING

Clavelin, Maurice. *The Natural Philosophy of Galileo*. Cambridge, Mass.: MIT Press, 1974.

Crew, Henry, & Alfonso de Salvio. *Galileo: Dialogues Concerning Two New Sciences*. New York: Dover, 1954.

Drake, Stillman. *Galileo: Dialogues Concerning the Two Chief World Systems*. Berkeley: University of California Press, 1953.

Drake, Stillman. *Discoveries & Opinions of Galileo*. New York: Doubleday, 1957. Contains *The Starry Messenger* and *The Assayer*.

Drake, Stillman. *Galileo at Work: His Scientific Biography*. Chicago: University of Chicago Press, 1978.

Finocchiaro, Maurice A. *Galileo and the Art of Reasoning*. Dordrecht: Reidel, 1980.

Finocchiaro, Maurice A. *The Galileo Affair: A Documentary History*. Berkeley: University of California Press, 1989.

Langford, Jerome J. *Galileo, Science and the Church*. Ann Arbor: University of Michigan Press, 1966.

McMullin, Ernan, ed. *Galileo: Man of Science*. New York: Basic Books, 1968.

Wallace, William A. *Prelude to Galileo: Essays on Medieval & Sixteenth-Century Sources of Galileo's Thought*. Boston: Reidel, 1981.

Weisheipl, James A. *Nature & Motion in the Middle Ages*. Washington: Catholic University of America Press, 1985.

THE ASSAYER

In accordance with the promise which I made to Your Excellency, I shall certainly state my ideas concerning the proposition "Motion is the cause of heat," explaining in what way it appears to me to be true. But first it will be necessary for me to say a few words concerning that which we call "heat," for I strongly suspect that the commonly held conception of the matter is very far from the truth, inasmuch as heat is generally believed to be a true accident, affection, or quality which actually resides in the material which we feel to be heated.

Now, whenever I conceive of any material or corporeal substance, I am necessarily constrained to conceive of that substance as bounded and as possessing this or that shape, as large or small in relationship to some other body, as in this or that place during this or that time, as in motion or at rest, as in contact or not in contact with some other body, as being one, many, or few—and by no stretch of imagination can I conceive of any corporeal body apart from these conditions. But I do not at all feel myself compelled to conceive of bodies as necessarily conjoined with such further conditions as being red or white, bitter or sweet, having sound or being mute, or possessing a pleasant or unpleasant fragrance. On the contrary, were they not escorted by our physical senses, perhaps neither reason nor understanding would ever, by themselves, arrive at such notions. I think, therefore, that these tastes, odors, colors,

etc., so far as their objective existence is concerned, are nothing
but mere names for something which resides exclusively in our
sensitive body (*corpo sensitivo*), so that if the perceiving creatures
were removed, all of these qualities would be annihilated and abol-
ished from existence. But just because we have given special names
to these qualities, different from the names we have given to the
primary and real properties, we are tempted into believing that the
former really and truly exist as well as the latter.

An example, I believe, will clearly explain my concept. Suppose
I pass my hand, first over a marble statue, then over a living man.
So far as the hand, considered in itself, is concerned, it will act in
an identical way upon each of these objects; that is, the primary
qualities of motion and contact will similarly affect the two objects,
and we would use identical language to describe this in each case.
But the living body, which I subject to this experiment, will feel
itself affected in various ways, depending upon the part of the body
I happen to touch; for example, should it be touched on the sole
of the foot or the kneecap, or under the armpit, it will feel, in
addition to simple contact, a further affection to which we have
given a special name: we call it "tickling." This latter affection is
altogether our own, and is not at all a property of the hand itself.
And it seems to me that he would be gravely in error who would
assert that the hand, in addition to movement and contact, intrinsi-
cally posesses another and different faculty which we might call the
"tickling faculty," as though tickling were a resident property of
the hand *per se*. Again, a piece of paper or a feather, when gently
rubbed over any part of our body whatsoever, will in itself act
everywhere in an identical way; it will, namely, move and contact.
But we, should we be touched between the eyes, on the tip of the
nose, or under the nostrils, will feel an almost intolerable titillation—while if touched in other places, we will scarcely feel anything at all. Now this titillation is completely ours and not the
feather's, so that if the living, sensing body were removed, nothing
would remain of the titillation but an empty name. And I believe
that many other qualities, such as taste, odor, color, and so on,
often predicated of natural bodies, have a similar and no greater
existence than this.

A solid body and, so to speak, one that is sufficiently heavy, when
moved and applied against any part of my body whatsoever, will
produce in me the sensation which we call "touch." Although this

sense is to be found in every part of the body, it appears principally to reside in the palm of the hand, and even more so in the fingertips, with which we can feel the minutest differences of roughness, texture, and softness and hardness—differences which the other parts of the body are less capable of distinguishing. Some amongst these tactile sensations are more pleasing than others, depending upon the differences of configuration of tangible bodies; that is to say, in accordance with whether they are smooth or irregular, sharp or dull, flexible or rigid. And the sense of touch, being more material than the other senses and being produced by the mass of the material itself, seems to correspond to the element of earth.

Since certain material bodies are continually resolving themselves into tiny particles, some of the particles, because they are heavier than air, will descend; and some of them, because they are lighter than air, will ascend. From this, perhaps, two further senses are born, for certain of the particles penetrate two parts of our body which are effectively more sensitive than the skin, which is incapable of feeling the incursion of materials which are too fine, subtle, or flexible. The descending particles are received by the upper surface of the tongue, and penetrating, they blend with its substance and moisture. Thus our tastes are caused, pleasant or harsh in accordance with variations in the contact of diversely shaped particles, and depending upon whether they are few or many, and whether they have high or low velocity. Other particles ascend, and entering the nostrils they penetrate the various nodes (*mammilule*) which are the instruments of smell; and these particles, in like manner through contact and motion, produce savoriness or unsavoriness—again depending upon whether the particles have this or that shape, high or low velocity, and whether they are many or few. It is remarkable how providently the tongue and nasal passages are situated and disposed, the former stretched beneath to receive the ingression of descending particles, and the latter so arranged as to receive those which ascend. The arrangement whereby the sense of taste is excited in us is perhaps analogous to the way in which fluids descend through the air, and the stimulation of the sense of smell may be compared to the manner in which flames ascend in it.

There remains the element of air, which corresponds to the sense of sound. Sounds come to us indiscriminately, from above and below and from either side, since we are so constituted as to be equally disposed to every direction of the air's movement; and the ear is so situated as to accommodate itself in the highest possible degree to any position in space. Sounds, then, are produced in us and felt when (without any special quality of harmoniousness or dissonance) there is a rapid vibration of air, forming minutely small waves, which move certain cartilages of a certain drum which is in our ear. The various external ways in which this wave-motion of the air is produced are manifold, but can in large part be reduced to the vibrating of bodies which strike the air and form the waves which spread out with great velocity. High frequencies give rise to high tones; low frequencies give rise to low tones, but I cannot believe that there exists in external bodies anything, other than their size, shape, or motion (slow or rapid), which could excite in us our tastes, sounds, and odors. And indeed I should judge that, if ears, tongues, and noses be taken away, the number, shape, and motion of bodies would remain, but not their tastes, sounds, and odors. The latter, external to the living creature, I believe to be nothing but mere names, just as (a few lines back) I asserted tickling and titillation to be, if the armpit or the sensitve skin inside the nose were removed. As to the comparison between the four senses which we have mentioned and the four elements, I believe that the sense of sight, most excellent and noble of all the senses, is like light itself. It stands to the others in the same measure of comparative excellence as the finite stands to the infinite, the gradual to the instantaneous, the divisible to the indivisible, the darkness to the light. Of this sense, and all that pertains to it, I can pretend to understand but little; yet a great deal of time would not suffice for me to set forth even this little bit that I know, or (to put it more exactly) for me to sketch it out on paper. Therefore I shall ponder it in silence.

I return to my first proposition, having now shown how some affections, often reputed to be indwelling properties of some external body, have really no existence save in us, and apart from us are mere names. I confess myself to be very much inclined to believe that heat, too, is of this sort, and that those materials which produce and make felt in us the sense of heat and to which we give the general name "fire" consist of a multitude of tiny particles of such and such a shape, and having such and such a velocity. These, when they encounter our body, penetrate it by means of their extreme subtlety; and it is their contact, felt by us in their passage through

our substance, which is the affection we call "heat." It will be pleas-
antly warm or unpleasantly hot depending upon the number and
the velocity (greater or lesser) of these pricking, penetrating particles—pleasant if by their penetration our necessary perspiring is
facilitated, unpleasant if their penetrating effects too great a division and dissolution of our substance. In sum, the operation of fire,
considered in itself, is nothing but movement, or the penetration
of bodies by its extreme subtlety, quickly or slowly, depending upon
the number and velocity of tiny corpuscles of flame (*ignicoli*) and
upon the greater or lesser density of the bodies concerned. Many
bodies dissolve in such a manner that the major part of them becomes transformed into further corpuscles of flame; and this dissolution continues as further dissolvable material is encountered.
But that there exists in fire, apart from shape, number, movement,
penetration, and contact, some further quality which we call "heat,"
I cannot believe. And I again judge that heat is altogether subjec-
tive, so that if the living, sensitive body be removed, what we call
heat would be nothing but a simple word. Since it is the case that
this affection is produced in us by passage of tiny corpuscles of
flame through our substance and their contact with it, it is obvious
that once this motion ceases, their operation upon us will be null.
It is thus that we perceive that a quantity of fire, retained in the
pores and pits of a piece of calcified stone, does not heat—even if
we hold it in the palm of our hand—because the flame remains
stationary in the stone. But should we swish the stone in water
where, because of its weight, it has greater propensity for movement and where the pits of the stone open somewhat, the corpuscles
of flame will escape and, encountering our hand, will penetrate it,
so that we will feel heat. Since, in order for heat to be stimulated
in us, the mere presence of corpuscles of flame is not by itself
sufficient, and since movement is required in addition, it is with
considerable reason that I declare motion to be the cause of heat.

This or that movement by which a scantling or other piece of
wood is burned up or by which lead and other metals are melted
will continue so long as the corpuscles of flame, moved either by
their own velocity or (if this be insufficient) aided by a strong blast
from a bellows, continue to penetrate the body in question; the
former will resolve itself into further corpuscles of flame or into
ash; the latter will liquify and be rendered fluid like water. From
a common-sense point of view, to assert that that which moves a

stone, piece of iron, or a stick, is what *heats* it, seems like an extreme vanity. But the friction produced when two hard bodies are rubbed together, which either reduces them to fine flying particles or permits the corpuscles of flame contained in them to escape, can finally be analyzed as motion. And the particles, when they encounter our body and penetrate and tear through it, are felt, in their motion and contact, by the living creature, who thus feels those pleasant or unpleasant affections which we call "heat," "burning," or "scorching."

Perhaps while this pulverizing and attrition continue, and remain confined to the particles themselves, their motion will be temporary and their operation will be merely that of heating. But once we arrive at the point of ultimate and maximum dissolution into truly indivisible atoms, light itself may be created, with an instantaneous motion or (I should rather say) an instantaneous diffusion and expansion, capable—I do not know if by the atoms' subtlety, rarity, immateriality, or by different and as yet unspecifiable conditions— capable, I say, of filling vast spaces.

But I should not like, Your Excellency, inadvertently to engulf myself in an infinite ocean without the means to find my way back to port. Nor should I like, while removing one doubt, to give birth to a hundred more, as I fear might in part be the case even in this timid venture from shore. Therefore, I shall await a more opportune moment to re-embark.

DIALOGUES CONCERNING THE TWO CHIEF WORLD SYSTEMS

THE SECOND DAY*

SALVIATI. Yesterday took us into so many and such great digressions twisting away from the main thread of our principal argument that I do not know whether I shall be able to go ahead without your assistance in putting me back on the track.
SAGREDO. I am not surprised that you should find yourself in some confusion, for your mind is as much filled and encumbered with

---

*Salviati represents the Copernican point of view; he is Galileo's mouthpiece. Simplicio represents the Aristotelian position. Sagredo is a supposedly neutral arbiter.

what remains to be said as with what has been said. But I am simply a listener and have in my mind only the things I have heard, so perhaps I can put your discourse back on its path by briefly outlining these for you.

As I recall it, yesterday's discourse may be summarized as a preliminary examination of the two following opinions as to which is the more probable and reasonable. The first holds the substance of the heavenly bodies to be ingenerable, incorruptible, inalterable, invariant, and in a word free from all mutations except those of situation, and accordingly to be a quintessence most different from our generable, corruptible, alterable bodies. The other opinion, removing this disparity from the world's parts, considers the earth to enjoy the same perfection as other integral bodies of the universe; in short, to be a movable and a moving body no less than the moon, Jupiter, Venus, or any other planet. Later many detailed parallels were drawn between the earth and the moon. More comparisons were made with the moon than with other planets, perhaps from our having more and better sensible evidence about the former by reason of its lesser distance. And having finally concluded this second opinion to have more likelihood than the other, it seems to me that our next step should be to examine whether the earth must be considered immovable, as most people have believed up to the present, or mobile, as many ancient philosophers believed and as others of more recent times consider it; and, if movable, what its motion may be.

SALV. Now I know and recognize the signposts along our road. But before starting in again and going ahead, I ought to tell you that I question this last thing you have said, about our having concluded in favor of the opinion that the earth is endowed with the same properties as the heavenly bodies. For I did not conclude this, just as I am not deciding upon any other controversial proposition. My intention was only to adduce those arguments and replies, as much on one side as on the other—those questions and solutions which others have thought of up to the present time (together with a few which have occurred to me after long thought)—and then to leave the decision to the judgment of others.

SAGR. I allowed myself to be carried away by my own sentiments, and believing that what I felt in my heart ought to be felt by others too, I made that conclusion universal which should have been kept particular. This really was an error on my part, especially as I do not know the views of Simplicio, here present.

SIMPLICIO. I confess that all last night I was meditating on yesterday's material, and truly I find it to contain many beautiful considerations which are novel and forceful. <u>Still, I am much more impressed by the authority</u> of so many great authors, and in particular . . . You shake your head, Sagredo, and smile, as if I had uttered some absurdity.

SAGR. I merely smile, but believe me, I am hardly able to keep from laughing, because I am reminded of a situation that I witnessed not many years ago together with some friends of mine, whom I could name to you for that matter.

SALV. Perhaps you had better tell us about it so that Simplicio will not go on thinking your mirth was directed at him.

SAGR. I'll be glad to. One day I was at the home of a very famous doctor in Venice, where many persons came on account of their studies, and others occasionally came out of curiosity to see some anatomical dissection performed by a man who was truly no less learned than he was a careful and expert anatomist. It happened on this day that he was investigating the source and origin of the nerves, about which there exists a notorious controversy between the Galenist and Peripatetic doctors. The anatomist showed that the great trunk of nerves, leaving the brain and passing through the nape, extended on down the spine and then branched out through the whole body, and that only a single strand as fine as a thread arrived at the heart. Turning to a gentleman whom he knew to be a Peripatetic philosopher, and on whose account he had been exhibiting and demonstrating everything with unusual care, he asked this man whether he was at last satisfied and convinced that the nerves originated in the brain and not in the heart. The philosopher, after considering for awhile, answered: "You have made me see this matter so plainly and palpably that if Aristotle's text were not contrary to it, stating clearly that the nerves originate in the heart, I should be forced to admit it to be true."

SIMP. Sir, I want you to know that this dispute as to the source of the nerves is by no means as settled and decided as perhaps some people like to think.

SAGR. Doubtless it never will be, in the minds of such opponents. But what you say does not in the least diminish the absurdity of this Peripatetic's reply; who, as a counter to sensible experience, adduced no experiment or argument of Aristotle's, but just the authority of his bare *ipse dixit*.

SIMP. Aristotle acquired his great authority only because of the strength of his proofs and the profundity of his arguments. Yet one must understand him, and not merely understand him, but have such thorough familiarity with his books that the most complete idea of them may be formed, in such a manner that every saying of his is always before the mind. He did not write for the common people, nor was he obliged to thread his syllogisms together by the trivial ordinary method; rather, making use of the permuted method, he has sometimes put the proof of a proposition among texts that seem to deal with other things. Therefore one must have a grasp of the whole grand scheme, and be able to combine this passage with that, collecting together one text here and another very distant from it. There is no doubt that whoever has this skill will be able to draw from his books demonstrations of all that can be known; for every single thing is in them.

SAGR. My dear Simplicio, since having things scattered all over the place does not disgust you, and since you believe by the collection and combination of the various pieces you can draw the juice out of them, then what you and the other brave philosophers will do with Aristotle's texts, I shall do with the verses of Virgil and Ovid, making centos of them and explaining by means of these all the affairs of men and the secrets of nature. But why do I speak of Virgil, or any other poet? I have a little book, much briefer than Aristotle or Ovid, in which is contained the whole of science, and with very little study one may form from it the most complete ideas. It is the alphabet, and no doubt anyone who can properly join and order this or that vowel and these or those consonants with one another can dig out of it the truest answers to every question, and draw from it instruction in all the arts and sciences. Just so does a painter, from the various simple colors placed separately upon his palette, by gathering a little of this with a bit of that and a trifle of the other, depict men, plants, buildings, birds, fishes, and in a word represent every visible object, without any eyes or feathers or scales or leaves or stones being on his palette. Indeed, it is necessary that none of the things imitated nor parts of them should actually be among the colors, if you want to be able to represent everything;

if there were feathers, for instance, these would not do to depict anything but birds or feather dusters.

SALV. And certain gentlemen still living and active were present when a doctor lecturing in a famous Academy, upon hearing the telescope described but not yet having seen it, said that the invention was taken from Aristotle. Having a text fetched, he found a certain place where the reason is given why stars in the sky can be seen during daytime from the bottom of a very deep well. At this point the doctor said: "Here you have the well, which represents the tube; here the gross vapors, from whence the invention of glass lenses is taken; and finally here is the strengthening of the sight by the rays passing through a diaphanous medium which is denser and darker."

SAGR. This manner of "containing" everything that can be known is similar to the sense in which a block of marble contains a beautiful statue, or rather thousands of them; but the whole point lies in being able to reveal them. Even better we might say that it is like the prophecies of Joachim or the answers of the heathen oracles, which are understood only after the events they forecast have occurred.

SALV. And why do you leave out the prophecies of the astrologers, which are so clearly seen in horoscopes (or should we say in the configurations of the heavens) after their fulfillment?

SAGR. It is in this way that the alchemists, led on by their madness, find that the greatest geniuses of the world never really wrote about anything except how to make gold; but in order to tell this without revealing it to the vulgar, this fellow in one manner and that one in another have whimsically concealed it under various disguises. And a very amusing thing it is to hear their comments upon the ancient poets, revealing the important mysteries hidden behind their stories—what the loves of the moon mean, and her descent to the earth for Endymion; her displeasure with Acteon; the significance of Jupiter's turning himself into a rain of gold, or into a fiery flame; what great secrets of the art there are in Mercury the interpreter, in Pluto's kidnapings, and in golden boughs.

SIMP. I believe, and to some extent I know, that the world does not lack certain giddy brains, but their folly should not redound to the discredit of Aristotle, of whom it seems to me you sometimes speak with too little respect. His antiquity alone, and the mighty name he has acquired among so many men of distinguished mind, should be enough to earn him respect among all the learned.

SALV. That is not quite how matters stand, Simplicio. Some of his followers are so excessively timid that they give us occasion (or more correctly would give us occasion if we credited their triflings) to think less of him. Tell me, are you so credulous as not to understand that if Aristotle had been present and heard this doctor who wanted to make him inventor of the telescope, he would have been much angrier with him than with those who laughed at this doctor and his interpretations? Is it possible for you to doubt that if Aristotle should see the new discoveries in the sky he would change his opinions and correct his books and embrace the most sensible doctrines, casting away from himself those people so weak-minded as to be induced to go on abjectly maintaining everything he had ever said? Why, if Aristotle had been such a man as they imagine, he would have been a man of intractable mind, of obstinate spirit, and barbarous soul; a man of tyrannical will who, regarding all others as silly sheep, wished to have his decrees preferred over the senses, experience, and nature itself. It is the followers of Aristotle who have crowned him with authority, not he who has usurped or appropriated it to himself. And since it is handier to conceal oneself under the cloak of another than to show one's face in open court, they dare not in their timidity get a single step away from him, and rather than put any alterations into the heavens of Aristotle, they want to deny out of hand those that they see in nature's heaven.

SAGR. Such people remind me of that sculptor who, having transformed a huge block of marble into the image of a Hercules or a thundering Jove, I forget which, and having with consummate art made it so lifelike and fierce that it moved everyone with terror who beheld it, he himself began to be afraid, though all its vivacity and power were the work of his own hands; and his terror was such that he no longer dared affront it with his mallet and chisel.

SALV. I often wonder how it can be that these strict supporters of Aristotle's every word fail to perceive how great a hindrance to his credit and reputation they are, and how the more they desire to increase his authority, the more they actually detract from it. For when I see them being obstinate about sustaining propositions which I personally know to be obviously false, and wanting to persuade me that what they are doing is truly philosophical and would be done by Aristotle himself, it much weakens my opinion that he philosophized correctly about other matters more recondite to me. If I saw them give in and change their opinions about obvious truths, I should believe that they might have sound proofs for those in which they persisted and which I did not understand or had not heard.

SAGR. Or truly, if it seemed to them that they staked too much of their own reputation and of Aristotle's in confessing that they did not know this or that conclusion discovered by someone else, would it not be a lesser evil for them to seek it among his texts by the collection of various of these according to the practice recommended by Simplicio? For if all things that can be known are in these texts, then it must follow that they can be discovered there.

SALV. Sagredo, do not sneer at this prudent scheme, which it seems to me you propose sarcastically. For it is not long since a famous philosopher composed a book on the soul in which, discussing Aristotle's opinion as to its mortality or immortality, he adduced many texts beyond those already quoted by Alexander. As to those, he asserted that Aristotle was not even dealing with such matters there, let alone deciding anything about them, and he gave others which he himself had discovered in various remote places and which tended to the damaging side. Being advised that this would make trouble for him in getting a license to publish it, he wrote back to his friend that he would nevertheless get one quickly, since if no other obstacle came up he would have no difficulty altering the doctrine of Aristotle; for with other texts and other expositions he could maintain the contrary opinion, and it would still agree with the sense of Aristotle.

SAGR. Oh, what a doctor this is! I am his to command; for he will not let himself be imposed upon by Aristotle, but will lead him by the nose and make him speak to his own purpose! See how important it is to know how to take time by the forelock! One ought not to get into the position of doing business with Hercules when he is under the Furies and enraged, but rather when he is telling stories among the Lydian maids.

Oh, the inexpressible baseness of abject minds! To make themselves slaves willingly; to accept decrees as inviolable; to place themselves under obligation and to call themselves persuaded and convinced by arguments that are so "powerful" and "clearly conclusive" that they themselves cannot tell the purpose for which they were written, or what conclusion they serve to prove! But let us call it a greater madness that among themselves they are even in doubt whether this very author held to the affirmative or the negative side. Now what is this but to make an oracle out of a log of wood, and run to it for answers; to fear it, revere it, and adore it?

SIMP. But if Aristotle is to be abandoned, whom shall we have for a guide in philosophy? Suppose you name some author.

SALV. We need guides in forests and in unknown lands, but on plains and in open places only the blind need guides. It is better for such people to stay at home, but anyone with eyes in his head and his wits about him could serve as a guide for them. In saying this, I do not mean that a person should not listen to Aristotle; indeed, I applaud the reading and careful study of his works, and I reproach only those who give themselves up as slaves to him in such a way as to subscribe blindly to everything he says and take it as an inviolable decree without looking for any other reasons. This abuse carries with it another profound disorder, that other people do not try harder to comprehend the strength of his demonstrations. And what is more revolting in a public dispute, when someone is dealing with demonstrable conclusions, than to hear him interrupted by a text (often written to some quite different purpose) thrown into his teeth by an opponent? If, indeed, you wish to continue in this method of studying, then put aside the name of philosophers and call yourselves historians, or memory experts; for it is not proper that those who never philosophize should usurp the honorable title of philosopher.

But we had better get back to shore, lest we enter into a boundless ocean and not get out of it all day. So put forward the arguments and demonstrations, Simplicio—either yours or Aristotle's—but not just texts and bare authorities, because our discourses must relate to the sensible world and not the one on paper. And since in yesterday's argument the earth was lifted up out of the darkness and exposed to the open sky, and the attempt to number it among the bodies we call heavenly was shown to be not so hopeless and prostrate a proposition that it remained without a spark of life, we should follow this up by examining that other proposition which holds it to be probable that the earth is fixed and utterly immovable as to its entire globe, and see what chance there is of making it movable, and with what motion.

Now because I am undecided about this question, whereas *Simplicio* has his mind made up with Aristotle on the side of immovability, he shall give the reasons for his opinion step by step, and I the answers and the arguments of the other side, while Sagredo shall tell us the workings of his mind and the side toward which he feels it drawn.

SAGR. That suits me very well, provided that I retain the freedom to bring up whatever common sense may dictate to me from time to time.

SALV. Indeed, I particularly beg you to do so; for I believe that writers on the subject have left out few of the easier and, so to speak, more material considerations, so that only those are lacking and may be wished for which are subtler and more recondite. And to look into these, what ingenuity can be more fitting than that of Sagredo's acute and penetrating wit?

SAGR. Describe me as you like, Salviati, but please let us not get into another kind of digression—the ceremonial. For now I am a philosopher, and am at school and not at court (*al Broio*).

SALV. Then let the beginning of our reflections be the consideration that whatever motion comes to be attributed to the earth must necessarily remain imperceptible to us and as if nonexistent, so long as we look only at terrestrial objects; for as inhabitants of the earth, we consequently participate in the same motion. But on the other hand it is indeed just as necessary that it display itself very generally in all other visible bodies and objects which, being separated from the earth, do not take part in this movement. So the true method of investigating whether any motion can be attributed to the earth, and if so what it may be, is to observe and consider whether bodies separated from the earth exhibit some appearance of motion which belongs equally to all. For a motion which is perceived only, for example, in the moon, and which does not affect Venus or Jupiter or the other stars, cannot in any way be the earth's or anything but the moon's.

Now there is one motion which is most general and supreme over all, and it is that by which the sun, moon, and all other planets and fixed stars—in a word, the whole universe, the earth alone excepted—appear to be moved as a unit from east to west in the space of twenty-four hours. This, in so far as first appearances are concerned, may just as logically belong to the earth alone as to the rest of the universe, since the same appearances would prevail as much in the one situation as in the other. Thus it is that Aristotle and Ptolemy, who thoroughly understood this consideration, in their attempt to prove the earth immovable do not argue against any other motion than this diurnal one, though Aristotle does drop a hint against another motion ascribed to it by an ancient writer, of which we shall speak in the proper place.

SAGR. I am quite convinced of the force of your argument, but it raises a question for me from which I do not know how to free myself, and it is this: Copernicus attributed to the earth another motion than the diurnal. By the rule just affirmed, this ought to remain imperceptible to all observations on the earth, but be visible in the rest of the universe. It seems to me that one may deduce as a necessary consequence either that he was grossly mistaken in assigning to the earth a motion corresponding to no appearance in the heavens generally, or that if the correspondent motion does exist, then Ptolemy was equally at fault in not explaining it away, as he explained away the other.

SALV. This is very reasonably questioned, and when we come to treat of the other movement you will see how greatly Copernicus surpassed Ptolemy in acuteness and penetration of mind by seeing what the latter did not—I mean the wonderful correspondence with which such a movement is reflected in all the other heavenly bodies. But let us postpone this for the present and return to the first consideration, with respect to which I shall set forth, commencing with the most general things, those reasons which seem to favor the earth's motion, so that we may then hear their refutation from Simplicio.

First, let us consider only the immense bulk of the starry sphere in contrast with the smallness of the terrestrial globe, which is contained in the former so many millions of times. Now if we think of the velocity of motion required to make a complete rotation in a single day and night, I cannot persuade myself that anyone could be found who would think it the more reasonable and credible thing that it was the celestial sphere which did the turning, and the terrestrial globe which remained fixed.

SAGR. If, throughout the whole variety of effects that could exist in nature as dependent upon these motions, all the same consequences followed indifferently to a hairsbreadth from both positions, still my first general impression of them would be this: I should think that anyone who considered it more reasonable for the whole universe to move in order to let the earth remain fixed would be more irrational than one who should climb to the top of your cupola just to get a view of the city and its environs, and then demand that the whole countryside should revolve around him so that he would not have to take the trouble to turn his head. Doubtless there are many and great advantages to be drawn from the new theory and not from the previous one (which to my mind is comparable with or even surpasses the above in absurdity), making the former more credible than the latter. But perhaps Aristotle, Ptolemy, and Simplicio ought to marshal their advantages against us and set them forth, too, if such there are; otherwise it will be clear to me that there are none and cannot be any.

· · · · ·

SAGR. If we do not want to repeat what happened yesterday, please get back to the point; and you, Simplicio, begin producing those difficulties that seem to you to contradict this new arrangement of the universe.

SIMP. The arrangement is not new; rather, it is most ancient, as is shown by Aristotle refuting it, the following being his refutations:

"First, whether the earth is moved either in itself, being placed in the center, or in a circle, being removed from the center, it must be moved with such motion by force, for this is not its natural motion. Because if it were, it would belong also to all its particles. But every one of them is moved along a straight line toward the center. Being thus forced and preternatural, it cannot be everlasting. But the world order is eternal; therefore, etc.

"Second, it appears that all other bodies which move circularly lag behind, and are moved with more than one motion, except the *primum mobile*. Hence it would be necessary that the earth be moved also with two motions; and if that were so, there would have to be variations in the fixed stars. But such are not to be seen; rather, the same stars always rise and set in the same place without any variations.

"Third, the natural motion of the parts and of the whole is toward the center of the universe, and for that reason also it rests therein." He then discusses the question whether the motion of the parts is toward the center of the universe or merely toward that of the earth, concluding that their own tendency is to go toward the former, and that only accidentally do they go toward the latter, which question was argued at length yesterday.

Finally he strengthens this with a fourth argument taken from experiments with heavy bodies which, falling from a height, go perpendicularly to the surface of the earth. Similarly, projectiles thrown vertically upward come down again perpendicularly by the same line, even though they have been thrown to immense height. These arguments are necessary proofs that their motion is toward the center of the earth, which, without moving in the least, awaits and receives them.

He then hints at the end that astronomers adduce other reasons in confirmation of the same conclusions—that the earth is in the center of the universe and immovable. A single one of these is that all the appearances seen in the movements of the stars correspond with this central position of the earth, which correspondence they would not otherwise possess. The others, adduced by Ptolemy and other astronomers, I can give you now if you like; or after you have said as much as you want to in reply to these of Aristotle.

SALV. The arguments produced on this matter are of two kinds. Some pertain to terrestrial events without relation to the stars, and others are drawn from the appearances and observations of celestial things. Aristotle's arguments are drawn mostly from the things around us, and he leaves the others to the astronomers. Hence it will be good, if it seems so to you, to examine those taken from earthly experiments, and thereafter we shall see to the other sort. And since some such arguments are adduced by Ptolemy, Tycho, and other astronomers and philosophers, in addition to their accepting, confirming, and supporting those of Aristotle, these may all be taken together in order not to have to give the same or similar answers twice. Therefore, Simplicio, present them, if you will; or, if you want me to relieve you of that burden, I am at your service.

SIMP. It will be better for you to bring them up, for having given them greater study you will have them readier at hand, and in great number too.

SALV. As the strongest reason of all is adduced that of heavy bodies, which, falling down from on high, go by a straight and vertical line to the surface of the earth. This is considered an irrefutable argument for the earth being motionless. For if it made the diurnal rotation, a tower from whose top a rock was let fall, being carried by the whirling of the earth, would travel many hundreds of yards to the east in the time the rock would consume in its fall, and the rock ought to strike the earth that distance away from the base of the tower. This effect they support with another experiment, which is to drop a lead ball from the top of the mast of a boat at rest, noting the place where it hits, which is close to the foot of the mast; but if the same ball is dropped from the same place when the boat is moving, it will strike at that distance from the foot of the mast which the boat will have run during the time of fall of the lead, and for no other reason than that the natural movement of the ball when set free is in a straight line toward the center of the earth. This argument is fortified with the experiment of a projectile sent a very great distance upward; this might be a ball shot from a cannon aimed perpendicular to the horizon. In its flight and return this consumes so much time that in our latitude the cannon and we would be carried together many miles eastward by the earth, so that the ball, falling, could never come back near the gun, but would fall as far to the west as the earth had run on ahead.

They add moreover the third and very effective experiment of shooting a cannon ball point-blank to the east, and then another one with equal charge at the same elevation to the west; the shot toward the west ought to range a great deal farther out than the other one to the east. For when the ball goes toward the west, and the cannon, carried by the earth, goes east, the ball ought to strike the earth at a distance from the cannon equal to the sum of the two motions, one made by itself to the west, and the other by the gun, carried by the earth, toward the east. On the other hand, from the trip made by the ball shot toward the east it would be necessary to subtract that which was made by the cannon following it. Suppose, for example, that the journey made by the ball in itself was five miles and that the earth in that latitude traveled three miles during the flight of the ball; in the shot toward the west, the ball would fall to earth eight miles distant from the gun—that is, its own five toward the west and the gun's three to the east. But the shot toward the east would range no further than two miles, which is all that remains after subtracting from the five of the shot the three of the gun's motion toward the same place. Now experiment shows the shots to fall equally; therefore the cannon is motionless, and consequently the earth is, too. Not only this, but shots to the south or north likewise confirm the stability of the earth; for they would never hit the mark that one had aimed at, but would always slant toward the west because of the travel that would be made toward the east by the target, carried by the earth while the ball was in the air. And not merely shots along the meridians, but even those made to the east or west would not range truly; for the easterly shots would carry high and the westerly low whenever they were aimed point-blank. Since the shots in both directions take the path of a tangent—that is, a line parallel to the horizon—and the horizon is always falling away to the east and rising in the west if the diurnal motion belongs to the earth (which is why the eastern stars appear to rise and the western stars to set), it follows that the target to the east would drop away under the shot, wherefore the shot would range high, and the rising of the western target would make the shot to the west low. Hence in no direction would shooting ever be accurate; and since experience is contrary to this, it must be said that the earth is immovable.

SIMP. Oh, these are excellent arguments, to which it will be impossible to find a valid answer.

. . . . .

SALV. Before going further I must tell Sagredo that I act the part of Copernicus in our arguments and wear his mask. As to the internal effects upon me of the arguments which I produce in his favor, I want you to be guided not by what I say when we are in the heat of acting out our play, but after I have put off the costume, for perhaps then you shall find me different from what you saw of me on the stage.

Now let us proceed. Ptolemy and his followers produce another experiment like that of the projectiles, and it pertains to things which, separated from the earth, remain in the air a long time, such as clouds and birds in flight. Since of these it cannot be said that they are carried by the earth, as they do not adhere to it, it does not seem possible that they could keep up with its swiftness; rather, it ought to look to us as if they were being moved very rapidly westward. If we, carried by the earth, pass along our parallel (which is at least sixteen thousand miles long) in twenty-four hours, how could the birds keep up on such a course? Whereas we see them fly east just as much as west or any other direction, without any detectable difference.

Besides this, if, when we travel on horseback, we feel the air strike rather strongly upon our faces, then what an east wind should we not perpetually feel when being borne in such a rapid course against the air! Yet no such effect is felt.

Here is another very ingenious argument taken from certain experiences. Circular motion has the property of casting off, scattering, and driving away from its center the parts of the moving body, whenever the motion is not sufficiently slow or the parts not too solidly attached together. If, for example, we should very rapidly spin one of those great treadmills with which massive weights are moved by one or more men walking within them (such as huge stones used in mangles, or barges being dragged across the land from one waterway to another), then if the parts of this rapidly turned wheel were not very solidly joined, it would all come apart. Or, if many rocks or other heavy materials were strongly attached to its external surface, they would not be able to resist the impetus, and it would scatter them with great force to various places far from the wheel, and accordingly from its center. If, then, the earth were to be moved with so much greater a velocity, what weight, what tenacity of lime or mortar would hold rocks, buildings and whole cities so that they would not be hurled into the sky by such precipitous whirling? And men and beasts, none of which are attached to the earth; how would they resist such an impetus? Whereas on the contrary, we see these and the much less resistant pebbles, sand, and leaves reposing quietly upon the earth, and even falling back upon it with very slow motion.

Here, Simplicio, are the very potent arguments taken, so to speak, from terrestrial things. There remain those of the other kind; that is, those with relation to celestial appearances, which arguments tend still more to show that the earth is in the center of the universe, and consequently deprive it of the annual motion around that center as attributed to it by Copernicus. These being of rather a different nature, they can be brought forth after we have judged the strength of those already propounded.

SAGR. Well, what do you say, Simplicio? Does it seem to you that Salviati understands and knows how to explain the Ptolemaic and Aristotelian arguments? Do you think any Peripatetic understands the Copernican proofs so well?

SIMP. Had I not formed from previous arguments such a high opinion of Salviati's soundness of learning and Sagredo's sharpness of wit, with their kind permission I should wish to leave without hearing any more, as it would appear to me an impossible feat to contradict such palpable experiences. And without hearing any more, I should like to cling to my old opinion; for it seems to me that if, indeed, it is false, it may be excused on the grounds of its being supported by so many arguments of such great probability. If these are fallacies, what true demonstrations were ever more elegant?

SAGR. Yet we had better listen to Salviati's answers, which if true must be even more beautiful; infinitely more beautiful, and the others extremely ugly, if that metaphysical proposition is correct which says that the true and the beautiful are one and the same, as are likewise the false and the ugly. Therefore, Salviati, let us not delay a moment more.

. . . . .

SALV. We may go on therefore to the fourth, with which it will be proper to deal at length, this being founded upon that experience from which most of the remaining arguments derive their force. Aristotle says, then, that a most certain proof of the earth's being motionless is that things projected perpendicularly upward are seen to return by the same line to the same place from which they were thrown, even though the movement is extrememly high. This, he argues, could not happen if the earth moved, since in the time during which the projectile is moving upward and then downward it is separated from the earth, and the place from which the pro-jectile began its motion would go a long way toward the east, thanks to the revolving of the earth, and the falling projectile would strike the earth that distance away from the place in question. Thus we can accommodate here the argument of the cannon ball as well as the other argument, used by Aristotle and Ptolemy, of seeing heavy bodies falling from great heights along a straight line perpendicular to the surface of the earth. Now, in order to begin to untie these knots, I ask Simplicio by what means he would prove that freely falling bodies go along straight and perpendicular lines directed toward the center, should anyone refuse to grant this to Aristotle and Ptolemy.

SIMP. By means of the senses, which assure us that the tower is straight and perpendicular, and which show us that a falling stone goes along grazing it, without deviating a hairsbreadth to one side or the other, and strikes at the foot of the tower exactly under the place from which it was dropped.

SALV. But if it happened that the earth rotated, and consequently carried along the tower, and if the falling stone were seen to graze the side of the tower just the same, what would its motion then have to be?

SIMP. In that case one would have to say "its motions," for there would be one with which it went from top to bottom, and another one needed for following the path of the tower.

SALV. The motion would then be a compound of two motions; the one with which it measures the tower, and the other with which it follows it. From this compounding it would follow that the rock would no longer describe that simple straight perpendicular line, but a slanting one, and perhaps not straight.

SIMP. I don't know about its not being straight, but I understand well enough that it would have to be slanting, and different from the straight perpendicular line it would describe with the earth motionless.

SALV. Hence just from seeing the falling stone graze the tower, you could not say for sure that it described a straight and perpendicular line, unless you first assumed the earth to stand still.

SIMP. Exactly so; for if the earth were moving, the motion of the stone would be slanting and not perpendicular.

SALV. Then here, clear and evident, is the paralogism of Aristotle and of Ptolemy, discovered by you yourself. They take as known that which is intended to be proved.

SIMP. In what way? It looks to me like a syllogism in proper form, and not a *petitio principii*.

SALV. In this way: Does he not, in his proof, take the conclusion as unknown?

SIMP. Unknown, for otherwise it would be superfluous to prove it.

SALV. And the middle term; does he not require that to be known?

SIMP. Of course; otherwise it would be an attempt to prove *ignotum per aeque ignotum*.

SALV. Our conclusion, which is unknown and is to be proved; is this not the motionlessness of the earth?

SIMP. That is what it is.

SALV. Is not the middle term which must be known, the straight and perpendicular fall of the stone?

SIMP. That is the middle term.

SALV. But wasn't it concluded a little while ago that we could not have any knowledge of this fall being straight and perpendicular unless it was first known that the earth stood still? Therefore in your syllogism, the certainty of the middle term is drawn from the uncertainty of the conclusion. Thus you see how, and how badly, it is a paralogism.

.   .   .   .   .

SAGR. I am content to excuse you from this recital for the time being, on condition that this shall be one of the propositions saved, among others, for examination in some special session, since such

information is highly desirable to me. In the meanwhile let us get
back to the line described by the body falling from the top of a
tower to its base.

SALV. If the straight movement toward the center of the earth were
uniform, and the circular motion toward the east were also uniform, the two could be compounded into a spiral line; one of those
defined by Archimedes in his book about the spirals bearing his
name, which are those generated when a point moves uniformly
along a straight line which is being uniformly rotated about a fixed
point at one of its extremities. But since the motion of the falling
weight is continually accelerated, the line compounded of the two
movements must have an ever-increasing ratio of successive distances from the circumference of that circle which would have been
marked out by the center of gravity of the stone had it always
remained on the tower. It is also required that this departure be
small at the beginning—or rather minimal, even the least possible.
For leaving from rest (that is, from the privation of downward
motion) and entering into motion straight down, the falling weight
must pass through every degree of slowness that exists between
rest and any speed of motion. These degrees are infinite, as was
discussed at length and decided already.

Supposing, then, that such is the progress of acceleraton; it being
further true that the descending weight tends to end at the center
of the earth, then the line of its compound motion must be such
as to travel away from the top of the tower at an ever-increasing
rate. To put it better, this line leaves from the circle described by
the top of the tower because of the revolution of the earth, its
departure from that circle being less *ad infinitum* according as the
moving body is found to be less and less removed from the point
where it was first placed. Moreover, this line of compound motion
must tend to terminate at the center of the earth. Now, making
these two assumptions, I draw the circle BI with A as a center and
radius AB, which represents the terrestrial globe. Next, prolonging
AB to C, the height of the tower BC is drawn; this, carried by the
earth along the circumference BI, marks out with its top the arc
CD.

Now dividing line CA at its midpoint E, and taking E as a center
and EC as radius, the semicircle CIA is described, along which I
think it very probable that a stone dropped from the top of the

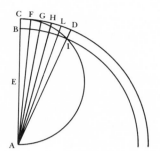

Fig. 1

tower C will move, with a motion composed of the general circular movement and its own straight one.

For if equal sections CF, FG, GH, HL are marked on the circumference CD, and straight lines are drawn to the center A from the points F, G, H, and L, the parts of these intercepted between the two circles CD and BI represent always the same tower CB, carried by the earth's globe toward DI. And the points where these lines are cut by the arc of the semicircle CA are the places at which the falling stone will be found at the various times. Now these points become more distant from the top of the tower in an ever-increasing proportion, and that is what makes its straight motion along the side of the tower show itself to be always more and more rapid. You may also see how, thanks to the infinite acuteness of the angle of contact between the two circles DC and CI, the departure of the stone from the circumference CFD (that is, from the top of the tower), is very, very small at the beginning, which is the same as saying that the downward motion is extremely slow; in fact, slower and slower *ad infinitum* according to its closeness to the point C, the state of rest. Finally, one may understand how such motion tends eventually to terminate at the center of the earth.

SAGR. I understand the whole thing perfectly, and I cannot think that the center of gravity of the falling body follows any other line but one such as this.

SALV. Hold on, Sagredo; I have also in store for you three little reflections of mine which may not displease you. The first is that if we consider the matter carefully, the body really moves in nothing other than a simple circular motion, just as when it rested on the tower it moved with a simple circular motion.

The second is even prettier; it moves not one whit more nor less than if it had continued resting on the tower; for the arcs CF, FG, GH, etc., which it would have passed through staying always on the tower, are precisely equal to the arcs of the circumference CI corresponding to the same CF, FG, GH, etc.

From this there follows a third marvel—that the true and real motion of the stone is never accelerated at all, but is always equable and uniform. For all these arcs marked equally on the circumference CD, and corresponding arcs marked on the circumference CI, are passed over in equal times. So we need not look for any other causes of acceleration or any other motions, for the moving body, whether remaining on the tower or falling, moves always in the same manner; that is, circularly, with the same rapidity, and with the same uniformity.

Now tell me what you think of these curiosities of mine.

SAGR. I tell you that I cannot find words to express the admiration they cause in me; and so far as my mind can make out at present, I do not believe that there is any other way in which these things can happen. I sincerely wish that all proofs by philosophers had half the probability of this one. Just to complete my satisfaction, I should like to hear the proof that those arcs are equal.

SALV. The demonstration is very easy. Suppose a line to be drawn from I to E; now the radius of the circle CD, that is the line CA, being double the radius CE of the circle CI, the circumference of the former will be double that of the latter, and every arc of the larger circle will be double the similar arc of the smaller. Thus half the arc of the larger circle is equal to the arc of the lesser. And since the angle CEI, made at the center E of the lesser circle and subtending the arc CI, is double the angle CAD, made at the center A of the larger circle and subtending the arc CD, then the arc CD is one-half of the arc in the larger circle similar to the arc CI. Hence the two arcs CD and CI are equal; and the same may be demonstrated in the same way for all the other parts. But that the descent of heavy bodies does take place in exactly this way, I will not at present declare; I shall only say that if the line described by a falling body is not exactly this, it is very near to it.

SAGR. Well, Salviati, there is another remarkable thing which I have just been reflecting about. It is that, according to these considerations, straight motion goes entirely out the window and nature never makes any use of it all. Even that use which you granted to it at the beginning, of restoring to their places such integral, natural bodies as were separated from the whole and badly disorganized, is now taken away and assigned to circular motion.

DISCOURSES CONCERNING THE TWO NEW SCIENCES

THE THIRD DAY

SALV. The present does not seem to be the proper time to investigate the cause of the acceleration of natural motion concerning which various opinions have been expressed by various philosophers, some explaining it by attraction to the center, others to repulsion between the very small parts of the body, while still others attribute it to a certain stress in the surrounding medium which closes in behind the falling body and drives it from one of its positions to another. Now, all these fantasies, and others too, ought to be examined; but it is not really worth while. At present it is the purpose of our Author merely to investigate and to demonstrate some of the properties of accelerated motion (whatever the cause of this acceleration may be)—meaning thereby a motion, such that the momentum of its velocity [*i momenti della sua velocita*] goes on increasing after departure from rest, in simple proportionality to the time, which is the same as saying that in equal time-intervals the body receives equal increments of velocity; and if we find the properties [of accelerated motion] which will be demonstrated later are realized in freely falling and accelerated bodies, we may conclude that the assumed definition includes such a motion of falling bodies and that their speed [*accelerazione*] goes on increasing as the time and the duration of the motion.

SAGR. So far as I see at present, the definition might have been put a little more clearly perhaps without changing the fundamental idea, namely, uniformly accelerated motion is such that its speed increases in proportion to the space traversed; so that, for example, the speed acquired by a body in falling four cubits would be double that acquired by a body falling two cubits and this latter speed would be double that acquired in the first cubit. Because there is no doubt but that a heavy body falling from the height of six cubits has, and strikes with, a momentum [*impeto*] double that it had at the end of three cubits, triple that which it had at the end of one.

SALV. It is very comforting to me to have had such a companion in error; and moreover let me tell you that your proposition seems so highly probable that our Author himself admitted, when I advanced this opinion to him, that he had for some time shared the same fallacy. But what most surprised me was to see two propositions so inherently probable that they commanded the assent of everyone to whom they were presented, proven in a few simple words to be not only false, but impossible.

SIMP. I am one of those who accept the proposition, and believe that a falling body acquires force [*vires*] in its descent, its velocity increasing in proportion to the space, and that the momentum [*momento*] of the falling body is doubled when it falls from a doubled height; these propositions, it appears to me, ought to be conceded without hesitation or controversy.

SALV. And yet they are as false and impossible as that motion should be completed instantaneously; and here is a very clear demonstration of it. If the velocities are in proportion to the spaces traversed, or to be traversed, then these spaces are traversed in equal intervals of time; if, therefore, the velocity with which the falling body traverses a space of eight feet were double that with which it covered the first four feet (just as the one distance is double the other) then the time-intervals required for these passages would be equal. But for one and the same body to fall eight feet and four feet in the same time is possible only in the case of instantaneous [discontinuous] motion; but observation shows us that the motion of a falling body occupies time, and less of it in covering a distance of four feet than of eight feet; therefore it is not true that its velocity increases in proportion to the space.

The falsity of the other proposition may be shown with equal clearness. For if we consider a single striking body the difference of momentum in its blows can depend only upon difference of velocity; for if the striking body falling from a double height were to deliver a blow of double momentum, it would be necessary for this body to strike with a doubled velocity; but with this doubled speed it would traverse a doubled space in the same time-interval; observation however shows that the time required for fall from the greater height is longer.

SAGR. You present these recondite matters with too much evidence and ease; this great fallacy makes them less appreciated than they would be had they been presented in a more abstruse manner. For, in my opinion, people esteem more lightly that knowledge which they acquire with so little labor than that acquired through long and obscure discussion.

SALV. If those who demonstrate with brevity and clearness the fallacy of many popular beliefs were treated with contempt instead of gratitude the injury would be quite bearable; but on the other hand it is very unpleasant and annoying to see men, who claim to be peers of anyone in a certain field of study, take for granted certain conclusions which later are quickly and easily shown by another to be false. I do not describe such a feeling as one of envy, which usually degenerates into hatred and anger against those who discover such fallacies; I would call it a strong desire to maintain old errors, rather than accept newly discovered truths. This desire at times induces them to unite against these truths, although at heart believing in them, merely for the purpose of lowering the esteem in which certain others are held by the unthinking crowd. Indeed, I have heard from our Academician many such fallacies held as true but easily refutable; some of these I have in mind.

SAGR. You must not withhold them from us, but, at the proper time, tell us about them even though an extra session be necessary. But now, continuing the thread of our talk, it would seem that up to the present we have established the definition of uniformly accelerated motion which is expressed as follows:

A motion is said to be equally or uniformly accelerated when, starting from rest, its momentum (*celeritatis momenta*) receives equal increments in equal times.

SALV. This definition established, the Author makes a single assumption, namely,

The speeds acquired by one and the same body moving down planes of different inclinations are equal when the heights of these planes are equal.

By the height of an inclined plane we mean the perpendicular let fall from the upper end of the plane upon the horizontal line drawn through the lower end of the same plane. Thus, to illustrate, let

the line AB be horizontal, and let the planes CA and CD be inclined
to it; then the Author calls the perpendicular CB the "height" of
the planes CA and CD; he supposes that the speeds acquired by
one and the same body, descending along the planes CA and CD
to the terminal points A and D are equal since the heights of these
planes are the same, CB; and also it must be understood that this
speed is that which would be acquired by the same body falling
from C to B.

SAGR. Your assumption appears to me so reasonable that it ought
to be conceded without queston, provided of course there are no
chance or outside resistances, and that the planes are hard and
smooth, and that the figure of the moving body is perfectly round,
so that neither plane nor moving body is rough. All resistance and
opposition having been removed, my reason tells me at once that
a heavy and perfectly round ball descending along the lines CA,
CD, CB would reach the terminal points A, D, B, with equal momenta [*impeti eguali*].

SALV. Your words are very plausible; but I hope by experiment to
increase the probability to an extent which shall be little short of a
rigid demonstration.

   Imagine this page to represent a vertical wall, with a nail driven
into it; and from the nail let there be suspended a lead bullet of
one or two ounces by means of a fine vertical thread, AB, say from
four to six feet long, on this wall draw a horizontal line DC, at right
angles to the vertical thread AB, which hangs about two finger-
breadths in front of the wall. Now bring the thread AB with the
attached ball into the position AC and set it free; first it will be
observed to descend along the arc CBD, to pass the point B, and
to travel along the arc BD, till it almost reaches the horizontal CD,
a slight shortage being caused by the resistance of the air and the
string; from this we may rightly infer that the ball in its descent
through the arc CB acquired a momentum [*impeto*] on reaching B,

Fig. 2

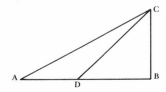

which was just sufficient to carry it through a similar arc BD to the same height. Having repeated this experiment many times, let us now drive a nail into the wall close to the perpendicular AB, say at E or F, so that it projects out some five or six finger-breadths in order that the thread, again carrying the bullet through the arc CB, may strike upon the nail E when the bullet reaches B, and thus compel it to traverse the arc BG, described about E as center. From this we can see what can be done by the same momentum [*impeto*] which previously starting at the same point B carried the same body through the arc BD to the horizontal CD. Now, gentlemen, you will observe with pleasure that the ball swings to the point G in the horizontal, and you would see the same thing happen if the obstacle were placed at some lower point, say at F, about which the ball would describe the arc BI, the rise of the ball always terminating exactly on the line CD. But when the nail is placed so low that the remainder of the thread below it will not reach to the height CD (which would happen if the nail were placed nearer B than to the intersection of AB with the horizontal CD) then the thread leaps over the nail and twists itself about it.

This experiment leaves no room for doubt as to the truth of our supposition; for since the two arcs CB and DB are equal and similarly placed, the momentum [*momento*] acquired by the fall through the arc CB is the same as that gained by fall through the arc DB; but the momentum [*momento*] acquired at B, owing to fall through CB, is able to lift the same body [*mobile*] through the arc BD; therefore, the momentum acquired in the fall BD is equal to that which

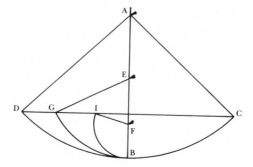

Fig. 3

lifts the same body through the same arc from B to D; so, in general, every momentum acquired by fall through an arc is equal to that which can lift the same body through the same arc. But all these momenta [*momenti*] which cause a rise through the arcs BD, BG, and BI are equal, since they are produced by the same momentum, gained by fall through CB, as experiment shows. Therefore all the momenta gained by fall through the arcs DB, GB, IB are equal.

SAGR. The argument seems to me so conclusive and the experiment so well adapted to establish the hypothesis that we may, indeed, consider it as demonstrated.

SALV. I do not wish, Sagredo, that we trouble ourselves too much about this matter, since we are going to apply this principle mainly in motions which occur on plane surfaces, and not upon curved, along which acceleration varies in a manner greatly different from that which we have assumed for planes.

So that, although the above experiment shows us that the descent of the moving body through the arc CB confers upon it momentum [*momento*] just sufficient to carry it to the same height through any of the arcs BD, BG, BI, we are not able, by similar means, to show that the event would be identical in the case of a perfectly round ball descending along planes whose inclinations are respectively the same as the chords of these arcs. It seems likely, on the other hand, that, since these planes form angles at the point B, they will present an obstacle to the ball which has descended along the chord CB, and starts to rise along the chord BD, BG, BI.

In striking these planes some of its momentum [*impeto*] will be lost and it will not be able to rise to the height of the line CD; but this obstacle, which interferes with the experiment, once removed, it is clear that the momentum [*impeto*] (which gains in strength with descent) will be able to carry the body to the same height. Let us then, for the present, take this as a postulate, the absolute truth of which will be established when we find that the inferences from it correspond to and agree perfectly with experiment.

Descartes

René Descartes was born in 1596 in the Brittany area of France. From 1604 to 1612 he was educated at the illustrious Jesuit college of La Flèche, where he met a fellow student, Father Marin Mersenne, who was to be his life-long friend and philosophical correspondent. After travel in Holland, Germany, and Italy, in 1628 he settled to a quiet life in Holland. There he proceeded to write major works in mathematics, philosophy, and science, and he carried on a voluminous correspondence with the major scholars of his day. In 1649 he went to Sweden to tutor Queen Christina, whose habit of 5 A.M. classes in the northern winter agreed more with her mind than with Descartes's body—he caught fever and died in February 1650.

Following upon some disturbing dreams in late 1619, Descartes's life work became the creation of a systematic philosophy which would encompass all branches of knowledge. The system would be based on a few undeniable principles, and all knowledge would be deduced from them, so that metaphysics, physics, mathematics, morals, and politics would all cohere. Knowledge is an organic whole, in which all fields have the same method. Descartes repeatedly used the metaphor of a tree:

> Thus philosophy as a whole is like a tree whose roots are metaphysics, whose trunk is physics, and whose branches, which issue from this trunk, are all the other sciences.[1]

This doctrine of a single, all-embracing method, is contrary to that of Aristotle, for whom the different fields of human knowledge all have their own subject matter and appropriate method.

Just like Francis Bacon, his contemporary in England, Descartes thought that a new beginning had to be made in human knowledge. The old philosophy of the Schools could not be reformed: Aristotelianism had to be rejected *in toto*. What survived from his schooling was an abiding enthusiasm and respect for mathematics, or, more specifically, Euclidean geometry. This was systematic, deductive, and methodical. From a few self-evident principles, knowledge of distant and complicated theorems could be generated, provided only that the correct method was followed.

Descartes was not the only person in the history of philosophy to be mesmerised by mathematics: to see in the structure, method, and certainty of mathematics the model for all human knowledge. Galileo and Newton were also convinced that physics (natural philosophy) should follow the geometrical method of analysis and synthesis.

Descartes's project was assisted by and perhaps indeed gave rise to his division of the world into mental and physical substances, thinking and corporeal substances. Physics dealt with corporeal substances. The nature and essence of corporeal substance, or matter, was 'extension in length, breadth, and depth.' Thus geometry was able to represent faithfully and without omission the very essence of the subject matter of physics. Physics could be geometrical. Just as Galileo before, and Robert Boyle and John Locke after, Descartes made a distinction between the primary and secondary qualities of matter. Colours, odours, heat were all the product of interaction between corporeal bodies and feeling subjects. Physics could ignore

---

1. "Author's Letter" for French translation of *Principles of Philosophy*

them. Physics was the science of determined, extended bodies in motion.

Along with Pierre Gassendi, Descartes revived corpuscularian philosophy.[2] The objects of experience—tables, chairs, stones— might be in essence extended and capable of geometrical repre- sentation, but what of the unseen and unseeable tiny corpuscles, the supposed building blocks of the universe? To these he assigns 'determinate figures, magnitudes and motions . . . as if I had seen them.'[3] There is clearly something of a leap of faith here, a leap made more perilous because Descartes so clearly wants certainty in his architectonic system of knowledge. What happens to the tree if the roots contain such a major unsupported hypothesis? Robert Boyle, another atomist, would later face the same question. De- pending upon answers to this question, different positions in epis- temology, or theory of knowledge, are derived. Instrumentalism, whereby theories such as the atomic hypothesis are believed not to tell us about unseen deep structures, but about how to manipulate surface events, is one answer; fallibilism, whereby theories are be- lieved to be about deep structures, but we only provisionally believe them until a better theory is developed, is another; absolutism, whereby we believe that our theories are true and will remain so, is yet another.

Hypotheses and experiments in science were matters of which Descartes had eventually to give an account. Some of the better known early works of his project—*Rules for the Direction of Mind* (1628), *Discourse on Method* (1637), *Meditations on First Philosophy* (1641)—were all to a large extent programmatic. (Of course other early works, such as the *Geometry*, *Opticks*, and *Meteorology*, were more specific and substantive.) These better known works were statements of an idea, expressions of a hope. There the vision of a deductive, coherent, certain body of all-encompassing knowledge could be safely entertained. But in his last major work, *The Principles of Philosophy* (1644), the promises had to be kept, the programme fulfilled, the vision given flesh. In the *Principles* he deals with sub- jects such as God's attributes, freedom of will, prejudice, laws of motion, laws of impact, planetary orbits, comets, rainbows, the

---

2. Descartes was an ambiguous corpuscularian. He did not believe in atoms, and he did not believe in a void. Atoms could always be further divided; space was everywhere filled.
3. *Principles of Philosophy*, § 203.

moon, the formation of mountains, tides, minerals, combustion, glass making, gravitation, magnets, and attraction in glass, etc. Indeed, so extensive is the list that Descartes claims for it 'That there is no phenomenon in nature which has not been dealt with in this treatise'.[4] Could he maintain his earlier confidence in a completely deductive, systematic, and certain science?

On the basis of the early methodological books, many see Descartes's science as entirely *a prioristic*. But clearly this cannot be so when the later *Principles* are considered. No one, not even Descartes, could pretend to spin out the explanation of mineral formation or the laws of free fall totally *a priori*. Guesses, hypotheses, experiments had to enter into the system at some place. How were these accommodated, given his concern for certainty and his goal of a systematic science?

Descartes's problem was recognised much earlier by Aristotle and by Thomas Aquinas: although one hypothesis might well account for the phenomena, so might many others.[5] To argue from an effect to a cause was always problematic unless one could, first, fully enumerate all the possible causes and, second, eliminate all but the chosen one. The second task is in practice difficult; the first is conceptually impossible. Aristotle called the problem the 'fallacy of affirming the consequent'.

Although the point is much debated, some see that logic and the complexity of experimentation forced Descartes in the end to moderate his epistemological position: certainty in science is given up in favour of fallibilism.[6] At the end of the *Principles*, he says he has done all that is required of him (and of science) if

> the causes I have assigned are such that they correspond to all the phenomena manifested by nature [without inquiring whether it is by their means or by others that they are produced].[7]

Descartes's relationship with Galileo is informative.[8] He knew of Galileo but does not mention him in his major works; comment is

---

4. *Principles of Philosophy*, § 199.
5. Thomas Gilby, *Saint Thomas Aquinas Philosophical Texts*, Oxford: Oxford University Press, 1951, p. 18.
6. See Daniel Garber, "Science and Certainty in Descartes," in Michael Hooker, ed., *Descartes: Critical & Interpretative Essays*, Baltimore: Johns Hopkins University Press, 1978, pp. 114–151.

confined to some letters. One in particular gives a good picture of Descartes's priorities, his views about the mathematising of physics and his commitment to a systematic philosophy. Writing to Mersenne (June 29, 1638), Descartes says of Galileo:

> I find that in general he philosophizes much better than the usual lot for he leaves as much as possible the errors of the School and strives to examine physical matters with mathematical reasons. In this I am completely in agreement with him and I hold that there is no other way of finding the truth. But I see a serious deficiency in his constant digressions and his failure to stop and explain a question fully. This shows that he has not examined them in order and that, without considering the first causes of nature, he has merely looked for the causes of some particular effects, and so has built without any foundation.[9]

It is most interesting that when Descartes dealt with the problem of free fall—a problem at the heart of physics since Aristotle's time—he repeated exactly the mistake that had so dogged the early attempts of Galileo to solve the problem. Everyone knew that bodies went faster as they fell, that they accelerated. Descartes assumed that acceleration uniformly increased with the distance traversed, rather than with the time elapsed. This mistake was so easy, so seemingly in accord with experience, yet it prevented Descartes's discovery of the law of free fall—distance traversed is as the square of time elapsed. This well illustrates the difficulty for the whole Cartesian programme, which depended upon not introducing any assumptions that were not absolutely certain and proven. Descartes's radical doubt did in fact leave many everyday assumptions untouched, assumptions so seemingly well-founded that they were not seriously examined.

One lasting and monumental scientific achievement of Descartes was his creation of analytic geometry. Up to his time, the mathematisation of science, so vital to the new science, meant the

---

7. *Principles of Philosophy*, § 204.
8. See William R. Shea, "Descartes as Critic of Galileo," in R.E. Butts & J.C. Pitt, eds., *New Perspectives on Galileo*, Dordrecht: Reidel, 1978, pp. 139–159. Also see Roger Ariew, "Descartes as Critic of Galileo's Scientific Methodology," *Synthese* 1986, 67 (1): 77–90.
9. In Shea, above, p. 148.

Archimedean-like rendering of scientific problems into Euclidean-geometric form. This was the method of Galileo. Distance (say) was represented by a line, time by another and solutions to unknowns were derived by geometric construction. Newton used this method in his *Principia*. In his *Geometry*, Descartes represented different line lengths by different variables, and converted geometry to algebra. Laborious proofs that took pages of Euclidean constructions were now reduced to a few clear, easy-to-follow algebraic steps. The long-hoped-for programme of mathematising science was now well and truly launched.

READING

Anscombe, E.S., and G.R.T. Ross, trans. *Descartes' Philosophical Writings*. London: Thomas Nelson, 1971.

Descartes, René. *Principles of Philosophy*. V.R. and R.P. Miller, trans. Dordrecht: Reidel, 1983.

Doney, W., ed. *Descartes: A Collection of Critical Essays*. London: Macmillan, 1967.

Gaukroger, S., ed. *Descartes: Philosophy, Mathematics and Physics*. Totowa, N.J.: Barnes & Noble, 1980.

Haldane, E.S. and G.R.T. Ross, trans. *The Philosophical Works of Descartes*. 2 vols., Cambridge: Cambridge University Press, 1911.

Hooker, M., ed. *Descartes' Critical and Interpretive Essays*. Baltimore: Johns Hopkins University Press, 1978.

Ree, J. *Descartes*. London: Penguin, 1974.

Vrooman, J.R. *René Descartes: A Biography*. New York: Putnam, 1970).

DISCOURSE ON THE METHOD OF RIGHTLY CONDUCTING THE REASON

But like one who walks alone and in the twilight I resolved to go so slowly, and to use so much circumspection in all things, that if my advance was but very small, at least I guarded myself well from falling. I did not wish to set about the final rejection of any single opinion which might formerly have crept into my beliefs without having been introduced there by means of Reason, until I had first of all employed sufficient time in planning out the task which I had undertaken, and in seeking the true Method of arriving at a knowledge of all the things of which my mind was capable.

Among the different branches of Philosophy, I had in my younger days to a certain extent studied Logic; and in those of Mathematics, Geometrical Analysis and Algebra—three arts or sciences which seemed as though they ought to contribute something to the design I had in view. But in examining them I observed in respect to Logic that the syllogisms and the greater part of the other teaching served better in explaining to others those things that one knows (or like the art of Lully, in enabling one to speak without judgment of those things of which one is ignorant) than in learning what is new. And although in reality Logic contains many precepts which are very true and very good, there are at the same time mingled with them so many others which are hurtful or superfluous, that it is almost as difficult to separate the two as to draw a Diana or a Minerva out of a block of marble which is not yet roughly hewn. And as to the Analysis of the ancients and the Algebra of the moderns, besides the fact that they embrace only matters the most abstract, such as appear to have no actual use, the former is always so restricted to the consideration of symbols that it cannot exercise the Understanding without greatly fatiguing the Imagination; and in the latter one is so subjected to certain rules and formulas that the result is the construction of an art which is confused and obscure, and which embarrasses the mind, instead of a science which contributes to its cultivation. This made me feel that some other Method must be found, which, comprising the advantages of the three, is yet exempt from their faults. And as a multiplicity of laws often furnishes excuses for evil-doing, and as a State is hence much better ruled when, having but very few laws, these are most strictly observed; so, instead of the great number of precepts of which Logic is composed, I believed that I should find the four which I shall state quite sufficient, provided that I adhered to a firm and constant resolve never on any single occasion to fail in their observance.

The first of these was to accept nothing as true which I did not clearly recognise to be so: that is to say, carefully to avoid precipitation and prejudice in judgments, and to accept in them nothing more than what was presented to my mind so clearly and distinctly that I could have no occasion to doubt it.

The second was to divide up each of the difficulties which I examined into as many parts as possible, and as seemed requisite in order that it might be resolved in the best manner possible.

The third was to carry on my reflections in due order, commencing with objects that were the most simple and easy to understand, in order to rise little by little, or by degrees, to knowledge of the most complex, assuming an order, even if a fictitious one, among those which do not follow a natural sequence relatively to one another.

The last was in all cases to make enumerations so complete and reviews so general that I should be certain of having omitted nothing.

Those long chains of reasoning, simple and easy as they are, of which geometricians make use in order to arrive at the most difficult demonstrations, had caused me to imagine that all those things which fall under the cognizance of man might very likely be mutually related in the same fashion; and that, provided only that we abstain from receiving anything as true which is not so, and always retain the order which is necessary in order to deduce the one conclusion from the other, there can be nothing so remote that we cannot reach to it, nor so recondite that we cannot discover it. And I had not much trouble in discovering which objects it was necessary to begin with, for I already knew that it was with the most simple and those most easy to apprehend. Considering also that of all those who have hitherto sought for the truth in the Sciences, it has been the mathematicians alone who have been able to succeed in making any demonstrations, that is to say producing reasons which are evident and certain, I did not doubt that it had been by means of a similar kind that they carried on their investigations.

PRINCIPLES OF PHILOSOPHY

Letter from the Author

Next, in order to give a clear conception of the aim which I had in publishing my writings, I should wish to explain here the order which it seems to me ought to be observed so that one may learn.

First, a man who thus far has only the common and imperfect knowledge which one can acquire in the four ways explained earlier must strive above all to form for himself a Moral code which can suffice to regulate the actions of his life; because that tolerates no delay, and because we must above all strive to live well. After that, he must also study Logic; not that of the schools, for that is properly speaking only a Dialectic which teaches the means of making others understand the things one knows, or even the means of speaking without judgment and at length about the things one does not know: as a consequence, that Logic corrupts rather than increases good sense. Rather, he must study that Logic which teaches how to use one's reason correctly in order to discover the truths of which one is ignorant; and because this depends greatly upon practice, he should drill himself for a long time by using the rules of Logic in relation to simple and easy questions, like those of Mathematics. Then, when he has become somewhat accustomed to discovering the truth in these questions, he must begin to apply himself seriously to true Philosophy, the first part of which is Metaphysics, which contains the Principles of knowledge; among which is the explanation of the principal attributes of God, of the immateriality of our souls, and of all the clear and simple notions which are in us. The second is Physics, in which, after having discovered the true Principles of material things, one examines, in general, the composition of the whole universe, and then, in particular, the nature of this Earth and of all the bodies which are most commonly found around it, like air, water, fire, the loadstone, and the other minerals. After this, it is also necessary to examine in particular the nature of plants, of animals, and above all, of man; in order to be capable of subsequently discovering all the other useful branches of knowledge. Thus, Philosophy as a whole is like a tree; of which the roots are Metaphysics, the trunk is Physics, and the branches emerging from this trunk are all the other branches of knowledge. These branches can be reduced to three principal ones, namely, Medicine, Mechanics, and Ethics (by which I mean the highest and most perfect Ethics, which presupposes a complete knowledge of the other branches of knowledge and is the final stage of Wisdom).

Now, just as it is not from the roots or from the trunk of trees that one gathers fruit, but only from the extremities of their branches, so the principal usefulness of Philosophy depends upon those parts of it which can only be learned last. But, although I am

ignorant of almost all of those, the zeal which I have always had
to strive to be of service to the public caused me to publish, ten or
twelve years ago, some essays on the things which it seemed to me
that I had learned. The first of these essays was a *Discourse on the
Method of rightly conducting one's reason and seeking truth in the sciences*,
in which I briefly stated the principal rules of Logic and of an
imperfect Ethics, which one can follow provisionally while one still
does not know anything better. The other essays were three treatises: the first *on Dioptrics*, the second *on Meteorology*, and the third
on Geometry. In the *Dioptrics*, it was my intention to show that one
can proceed far enough in Philosophy to achieve by its means a
knowledge of those arts which are useful to life, because the de-
signing of telescopes, which I explained there, is one of the most
difficult tasks ever undertaken. In the *Meteorology*, I wished to make
known the difference between the Philosophy which I study and
that which is taught in the schools where it is customary to treat of
the same subject. Finally, in the *Geometry*, I sought to demonstrate
that I had discovered many things which were previously unknown
and thus to provide grounds for believing that many others can
still be discovered, in order to thereby incite all men to the search
for truth. Subsequently, foreseeing the difficulty which many would
have in conceiving the foundations of Metaphysics, I attempted to
explain its principal points in a book of *Meditations* which is not
very long, but whose length was increased and subject matter much
illuminated by the objections concerning these *Meditations* which
several very learned persons sent to me, and by the responses which
I made to them. Then, finally, when it seemed to me that these
preceding treatises had sufficiently prepared the minds of Readers
to receive the *Principles of Philosophy*, I published these also; dividing
the Book into four parts, the first of which contains the Principles
of knowledge, which are what one can call first Philosophy or Metaphysics: that is why, in order to understand this first part well, it
is appropriate to read beforehand the Meditations which I wrote
on the same subject. The other three parts contain everything which
is most general in Physics, namely, the explanation of the first laws
or Principles of Nature, and the way in which the Heavens, the
fixed Stars, the Planets, the Comets, and generally all the universe
is composed; then, in particular, the nature of this earth, of air, of
water, of fire, and of the loadstone, which are the bodies one can
most commonly find everywhere about the earth; and of all the

qualities which are observed in these bodies, such as light, heat, weight, and similar things: by which means I believe I have begun to explain all Philosophy in correct order, without having omitted any of those things which ought to precede the last things which I wrote. However, in order to pursue this project to completion, I ought hereafter to explain in the same way the nature of each of the other even more particular bodies which are on the earth, namely, minerals, plants, animals, and, principally, man. Finally, I ought to treat accurately of Medicine, Ethics, and Mechanics. That is what I would have to do in order to give men a perfectly complete body of Philosophy: and I do not yet feel so old; I do not have so little trust in my strength; I do not judge myself so far from the knowledge of what remains; that I would not dare to undertake to complete this project if it were possible for me to perform all the experiments which I would need in order to support and justify my reasonings. But, perceiving that to do this would require great expenditures which a private individual like myself could not meet without the help of the public, and not perceiving that I should expect that help; I believe I must henceforth content myself with studying for my personal instruction and that posterity will pardon me if I cease henceforth to work in its behalf.

PART I

51   What substance is, and that this term does not apply univocally to God and to created things.

However, as for what we regard as things or as modes of things, it is worthwhile for us to consider them individually and separately here {in order to distinguish what is obscure from what is evident in our notion of them}. By *'substance'*, we can understand nothing other than a thing which exists in such a way that it needs no other thing in order to exist. And indeed only one substance which needs absolutely no other thing can be understood; i.e., God. We perceive that, on the contrary, all others can exist only with the aid of God's participation. And consequently the term 'substance' does not apply to God and to those other things "univocally" (as is customarily {and rightly} said in the Schools), that is, no meaning of this term can distinctly be understood which is common to God and to created things. {But because, among created things, some are such that they cannot exist without some others; we distinguish them from

those which require only the normal participation of God by nam-
ing the latter substances and the former the qualities or attributes
of these substances}.

52   That the term 'substance' is univocally applicable to mind and body; and how substance is known.

However, corporeal substance and created mind, or thinking substance, can be understood from this common concept: that they
are things which need only the participation of God in order to
exist. Yet substance cannot be initially perceived solely by means
of the fact that it is an existing thing, for this fact alone does not
per se affect us;[1] but we easily recognize substance from any atttri-
bute of it, by means of the common notion that nothingness has
no attributes and no properties or qualities. For, from the fact that
we perceive some attribute to be present, we {rightly} conclude that
some existing thing, or substance, to which that attribute can belong, is also necessarily present.

53   That each substance has one principal attribute, thought, for example, being that of mind, and ex-tension that of body.

And substance is indeed known by any attribute [of it]; but each
substance has only one principal property which constitutes its nature and essence, and to which all the other properties are related.
Thus, extension in length, breadth, and depth constitutes the nature of corporeal substance; and thought constitutes the nature of
thinking substance. For everything else which can be attributed to
body presupposes extension, and is only a certain mode {or de-
pendence} of an extended thing; and similarly, all the properties
which we find in mind are only diverse modes of thinking. Thus,
for example, figure cannot be understood except in an extended
thing, nor can motion, except in an extended space; nor can imagination, sensation, or will, except in a thinking substance. But on

---

1. The French text is quite different here: "But when it comes to knowing whether
one of these substances truly exists, that is, whether it is at present in the world,
the fact that it exists without the aid of any created thing is not sufficient to cause
us to perceive it; for that fact alone does not reveal to us anything which excites
some specific knowledge in our mind."

the contrary, extension can be understood without figure or motion; and thought without imagination or sensation, and so on; as is obvious to anyone who pays attention to these things.

PART II

36 That God is the primary cause of motion; and that He always maintains an equal quantity of it in the universe.

After having examined the nature of movement, we must consider its cause, which is twofold: {we shall begin with} the universal and primary one, which is the general cause of all the movements in the world; and then {we shall consider} the particular ones, by which individual parts of matter acquire movements which they did not previously have. As far as the general {and first} cause is concerned, it seems obvious to me that this is none other than God Himself, who, {being all-powerful} in the beginning created matter with both movement and rest; and now maintains in the sum total of matter, by His normal participaton, the same quantity of motion and rest as He placed in it at that time.[1] For although motion is only a mode of the matter which is moved, nevertheless there is a fixed and determined quantity of it; which, as we can easily understand, can be always the same in the universe as a whole even though there may at times be more or less motion in certain of its individual parts. That is why we must think that when one part of matter moves twice as fast as another twice as large, there is as much motion in the smaller as in the larger; and that whenever the movement of one part decreases, that of another increases exactly in proportion. We also understand that it is one of God's perfections to be not only immutable in His nature, but also immutable and com-

---

1. It is important to note here that by 'quantity of motion' Descartes does not mean momentum, i.e., mass times velocity. Rather, he intends quantity of motion to be given by the product of size (or volume) and speed. This is, of course, a result of his view that extension is the essential property of matter. Thus, the behavior of bodies should be determined entirely by their extension, figure, and motion (figure and motion being essential attributes of extended things). The preference of speed over velocity may result from the claim that the direction in which a body moves depends upon which other bodies are considered at rest. Therefore, there is nothing *in the body itself* which enables one to determine its direction of motion.

pletely constant in the way He acts. Thus, with the exception of those changes which either manifest experience or divine revelation renders certain, and which we either perceive or believe to occur without any change on the part of the Creator; we must not suppose that there are any others in His works, for fear of accusing Him of inconstancy. From this it follows that it is completely consistent with reason for us to think that, solely because God moved the parts of matter in diverse ways when He first created them, and still maintains all this matter exactly as it was at its creation, and subject to the same law as at that time; He also always maintains in it an equal quantity of motion.[2]

37 The first law of nature: that each thing, as far as is in its power,[3] always remains in the same state; and that consequently, when it is once moved, it always continues to move.

Furthermore, from this same immutability of God, we can obtain knowledge of the rules or laws of nature, which are the secondary and particular causes of the diverse movements which we notice in individual bodies. The first of these laws is that each thing, provided that it is simple and undivided, always remains in the same state as far as is in its power, and never changes except by external causes. Thus, if some part of matter is square, we are easily convinced that it will always remain square unless some external intervention changes its shape. Similarly, if it is at rest, we do not believe that it will ever begin to move unless driven to do so by some external cause. Nor, if it is moving, is there any significant reason to think that it will ever cease to move of its own accord and without some other thing which impedes it. We must therefore conclude that whatever is moving always continues to move as far as is in its power. However, because we inhabit the earth, which is so constituted that all movements which occur near to it cease in a short while (and

2. While this may be consistent with reason, it clearly does not follow. What follows, even on the most generous interpretation, is that the total quantity of *something* must remain constant. There was considerable subsequent dispute between the adherents of Descartes and those of Leibniz as to whether quantity of motion or what we now know as quantity of energy was conserved. In fact, if quantity of motion is taken to mean momentum, both are conserved.

3. Latin'*quantum in se est*'; 'as far as is in its power' or 'as far as it [itself] is concerned'.

frequently from causes which are concealed from our senses), we often judged, from the beginning of our life, that those movements which thus ceased for reasons unknown to us, did so of their own accord. Indeed, because experience seems to have proved it to us on many occasions, we are still inclined to believe that all movements cease by virtue of their own nature, or that bodies have a tendency toward rest. Yet this is assuredly in complete contradiction with the laws of nature; for rest is the opposite of movement, and nothing moves by virtue of its own nature toward its opposite or its own destruction.[4]

38 Why bodies which have been thrown continue to move after they leave the hand.[5]

Indeed, daily experience of things which are thrown to a distance confirms this {first} rule in every way. For there is no other reason why things which have been thrown should continue to move for some time after they have left the hand which threw them except that, {in accordance with the laws of nature}, having once begun to move, they continue to do so until they are slowed down by encounter with other bodies. It is obvious, moreoever, that they are always gradually slowed down, either by the air itself or by some other fluid bodies through which they are moving, and that, as a result, their movement cannot last for long. We can in fact prove by our own sense of touch that the air resists the movement of other bodies, if we shake an {open} fan vigorously. The flight of birds confirms the same thing.[6] Moreover, there is no other fluid body {on the earth} which does not resist the movement of projectiles even more manifestly than does the air.

---

4. Descartes's rejection of this view is associated with his rejection of final causes in general (see Part I, Article 28). The overthrow of the Ancient Greek view that change was to be understood in terms of an inner tendency or nature of the changing thing and the realization that change only results from some sort of interaction were essential ingredients of the scientific revolution.

5. This was one of the most difficult problems of Aristotelian physics. Since heavy objects had an innate tendency toward rest and since nothing appeared to be pushing a projectile, it was difficult to explain what was overcoming the body's natural tendency.

6. Presumably, because if the air did not resist the motion of the bird's wings, it would simply fall to Earth. The French text omits this sentence.

39 The second law of nature: that all movement is, of itself, along straight lines;[7] and consequently, bodies which are moving in a circle always tend to move away from the center of the circle which they are describing.

The second law of nature {which I observe} is: that each part of matter, considered individually, tends to continue its movement only along straight lines, and never along curved ones; even though many of these parts are frequently forced to move aside because they encounter others in their path, and even though, as stated before, in any movement, a circle of matter which moves together is always in some way formed. This rule, like the preceding one, results from the immutability and simplicity of the operation by which God maintains movement in matter; for He only maintains it precisely as it is at the very moment at which He is maintaining it, and not as it may perhaps have been at some earlier time. Of course, no movement is accomplished in an instant; yet it is obvious that every moving body, at any given moment in the course of its movement, is inclined to continue that movement in some direction in a straight line, and never in a curved one. For example, when the stone A is rotated in the sling EA[8] and describes the circle ABF; at the instant at which it is at point A, it is inclined to move along the tangent of the circle toward C. We cannot conceive that it is inclined to any circular movement: for although it will have previously come from L to A along a curved line, none of this circular movement can be understood to remain in it when it is at point A. Moreover, this is confirmed by experience, because if the stone then leaves the sling, it will continue to move, not toward B, but toward C. From this it follows that any body which is moving in a circle constantly tends to move [directly] away from the center of the circle which it is describing. Indeed, our hand can even feel

---

7. The previous law, combined with the first portion of this one, is generally regarded as the first statement of what was to become Newton's law of inertia. There is a significant difference in import between Newton's view and Descartes's, however. Whereas Newton regards motion and rest as merely quantitatively different; Descartes regards them as *opposite* or opposing states. See Articles 44, 49, and 50.
8. See Fig. i.

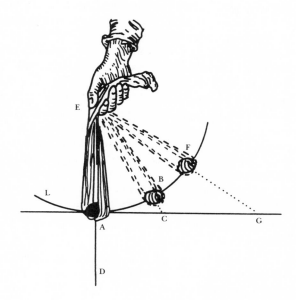

Fig. i

this while we are turning the stone in the sling, {for it pulls and stretches the rope in an attempt to move away from our hand in a straight line}.[9] This consideration {is of such importance, and} will be so frequently used in what follows, that it must be very carefully noticed here; I shall explain it more fully later.

40   The third law: that a body upon coming in contact with a stronger one, loses none of its motion; but that, upon coming in contact with a weaker one, it loses as much as it transfers to that weaker body.[10]

This is the third law of nature: when a moving body meets another, if it has less force to continue to move in a straight line than the

9. The force described here is known as 'centrifugal force'; a term introduced by Huygens. This force forms the basis of Descartes's planetary mechanics and his explanation of the phenomenon of light in Part III. Unfortunately, with regard to the stone, the force is nonexistent. See the extensive commentary to Articles 57 and 58 of Part III.

10. This apparently innocent law might appear to be a rather trivial consequence

other has to resist it, it is turned aside in another direction, retaining its quantity of motion and changing only the direction of that motion. If, however, it has more force; it moves the other body with it, and loses as much of its motion as it gives to that other. Thus, we know from experience that when any hard bodies which have been set in motion strike an unyielding body, they do not on that account cease moving, but are driven back in the opposite direction; on the other hand, however, when they strike a yielding body to which they can easily transfer all their motion, they immediately come to rest. All the individual causes of the changes which occur in [the motion of] bodies are included under this third law, or at least those causes which are physical; for I am not here enquiring into what kind of power the minds of men or Angels may perhaps have to move bodies; I am reserving that matter for a treatise *on man*.

64   That I do not accept or desire in Physics any other principles than in Geometry or abstract Mathematics; because all the phenomena of nature are explained thereby, and certain demonstrations concerning them can be given.

I shall not add anything here concerning figures, or the way in which there also result, from their infinite diversity, innumerable diversities of movement; because these things will be, of themselves, sufficiently obvious when the occasion to discuss them arises. Furthermore, I am supposing that my readers are already familiar with the rudiments of Geometry, or that they at least have capacities adequate to the understanding of Mathematical demonstrations. For I openly acknowledge that I know of no kind of material substance other than that which can be divided, shaped, and moved in every possible way, and which Geometers call quantity and take as the object of their demonstrations. And [I also acknowledge] that there is absolutely nothing to investigate about this substance except those divisions, shapes, and movements; and that nothing con-

---

of the law of conservation of motion, and it can be so regarded if the meanings of 'stronger' and 'weaker' are left sufficiently vague. When Descartes specifies the conditions under which a body will be weaker or stronger than another, thereby specifying the meaning of those terms, this law becomes one of the principal sources of error in his physics. See esp. Articles 46–52.

cerning these can be accepted as true unless it is deduced from common notions, whose truth we cannot doubt, with such certainty that it must be considered as a Mathematical demonstration. And because all Natural Phenomena can thus be explained, as will appear in what follows; I think that no other principles of Physics should be accepted, or even desired.

PART IV

198 That we perceive by our senses nothing in external objects except their figures, sizes, and movements.

Furthermore, we do not perceive any differences between nerves from which it might be permissible to judge that there is anything which reaches the brain (from the organs of the external senses) through some nerves but not through others; or that anything other than local movement of these nerves reaches it at all.[1] And we see that this local movement not only produces the feeling of titillation or pain, but also that of light and sounds. For if anyone is struck in the eye in such a way that the vibration of the blow reaches the retina, that alone will cause him to see very many sparks of flashing light which will not be outside the eye. And if someone stops up his ear with a finger, he will hear a certain tremulous murmur, which will result solely from the movement of the air trapped in the ear. Finally, we often notice that heat and other perceptible qualities, insofar as they are in objects, and also the forms of purely material things (as for example, the form of fire), arise from the local movement of certain bodies, and that these then themselves cause other local movements in other bodies. And we very well comprehend how the various sizes, figures, and movements of the particles of one body produce various local movements in another body. However, we cannot in any way comprehend how the same things (that is, size, figure, and movement) can produce something else of an entirely different nature from themselves, such as those substantial forms and real qualities which many {Philosophers} suppose to be in things; nor indeed how, subsequently, these qualities or forms can have the force to excite local movement in other

---

1. In the *Dioptrics*, Descartes implies that differences between sensations are due to the different locations of the nerve-endings in the brain and to the different sorts of movements transmitted by the nerves; see Discourses IV and VI.

bodies. Since this is so, and since we know it to be the nature of
our soul that diverse local movements suffice to provoke in it all
feelings; and since we know by experience that those various feelings are in fact aroused in it, and do not perceive that anything
other than movements of this kind travels to the brain from the
organs of the external senses: it must certainly be concluded regarding those things which, in external objects, we call by the names
of light, color, odor, taste, sound, heat, cold, and of other tactile
qualities, or else [by the names] of substantial forms; that we are
not aware of their being anything other than various arrangements
{of the size, figure, and motions of the parts} of these objects which
make it possible for our nerves to move in various ways, {and to
excite in our soul all the various feelings which they produce there}.

199   That no phenomena of nature have been omitted in this treatise.

And thus, by simple enumeration, it is concluded that no phenomena of nature have been omitted by me in this treatise. For
nothing is to be numbered among the phenomena of nature, except
what is perceived by the senses. However, apart from size, figure,
and motion, [the varieties of] which I have explained as they are
in each body, nothing located outside us is observed except light,
color, odor, taste, sound, and tactile qualities; which I have now
demonstrated are nothing in the objects other than, or at least are
perceived by us as nothing other than, certain dispositions of size,
figure, and motion {of bodies. Thus, . . . there is nothing visible or
perceptible in this world that I have not explained}.

203   How we know the figures and movements of imperceptible particles.

But I attribute determined figures, and sizes, and movements to
the imperceptible particles of bodies, as if I had seen them; and
yet I acknowledge that they are imperceptible. And on that account,
some readers may perhaps ask how I therefore know what they
are like. To which I reply: that I first generally considered, from
the simplest and best known principles (the knowledge of which is
imparted to our minds by nature), what the principal differences
in the sizes, figures, and situations of bodies which are imperceptible solely on account of their smallness could be, and what perceptible effects would follow from their various encounters. And

next, when I noticed some similar effects in perceptible things, I judged that these things had been created by similar encounters of such imperceptible bodies; especially when it seemed that no other way of explaining these things could be devised. And, to this end, things made by human skill helped me not a little: for I know of no distinction between these things and natural bodies, except that the operations of things made by skill are, for the most part, performed by apparatus large enough to be easily perceived by the senses: for this is necessary so that they can be made by men. On the other hand, however, natural effects almost always depend on some devices so minute that they escape all senses. And there are absolutely no judgments {or rules} in Mechanics which do not also pertain to Physics, of which Mechanics is a part or type: and it is as natural for a clock, composed of wheels of a certain kind, to indicate the hours, as for a tree, grown from a certain kind of seed, to produce the corresponding fruit. Accordingly, just as when those who are accustomed to considering automata know the use of some machine and see some of its parts, they easily conjecture from this how the other parts which they do not see are made: so, from the perceptible effects and parts of natural bodies, I have attempted to investigate the nature of their causes and of their imperceptible parts.

204 That it suffices if I have explained what imperceptible things may be like, even if perhaps they are not so.

And although perhaps in this way it may be understood how all natural things could have been created, it should not therefore be concluded that they were in fact so created. For just as the same artisan can make two clocks which indicate the hours equally well and are exactly similar externally, but are internally composed of an entirely dissimilar combination of small wheels: so there is no doubt that the greatest Artificer of things could have made all those things which we see in many diverse ways. And indeed I most willingly concede this to be true, and will think that I have achieved enough if those things which I have written are only such that they correspond accurately to all the phenomena of nature, {whether these effects are produced by the causes I have explained or by others}. And indeed this will also suffice for the needs of everyday life, because Medicine and Mechanics, and all the other arts which can be perfected with the help of Physics, have as their goal only those effects which are perceptible and which accordingly ought to be numbered among the phenomena of nature. {And if these [desired] phenomena are produced by considering the consequences of some causes thus imagined, although false; we shall do as well as if these were the true causes, since the result is assumed similar as far as the perceptible effects are concerned}. And lest by chance anyone should believe that Aristotle ever achieved, or sought to achieve, anything more; he himself in the first book of the *Meteorology* at the beginning of Chapter 7, clearly asserts, concerning things which are not evident to the senses, that he thinks he is giving sufficient reasons and demonstrations if he only shows that these can be created as they are explained by him.

Boyle

Of the Excellency and Grounds of the Corpuscular or Mechanical Hypothesis (1674)

(corpuscularian philosophy, criticism of Aristotelian science)

Robert Boyle was born in 1627. As a precocious teenager, he was in Florence reading Galileo at the time of the latter's death; his early works as a gentleman of leisure were on ethics and theology. Increasingly he turned to natural science and came into close contact with philosophers and scientists who were to found the Royal Society in 1663. For the next three decades he produced a new science of chemistry and advanced the philosophy of corpuscularianism as the most fitting philosophical base for the new science of his age. He died in 1691. His life was almost coterminous with those of Christian Huygens, Robert Hooke, Isaac Newton, and John Locke. He was one of the jewels of the late English Renaissance.

It is standard to date modern chemistry from 1660, the year of Boyle's *The Skeptical Chymist*. In this book Boyle rejected the Aristotelian assumption of forms being responsible for chemical changes and the doctrine of the four basic elements: earth, fire, water, and air. He also rejected the alchemy of Paracelus, for its lack of systematic theory, and the work of some contemporary chemists, which was based on an assumption of three prime elements: salt, sulphur, and mercury.

Because chemistry dealt directly with the properties of matter, Boyle thought it ought to have a privileged place in the curriculum of natural philosophy. *The Origin of Forms and Qualities* (1666) well illustrates how he used science as a tool in philosophical argument. At the end of a litany of experimental results, he concluded that

109

neither Aristotelian substantial forms nor the principles of his contemporary chemists were adequate for the explanatory job at hand.
Instead he advocated basing chemistry on the 'catholic and fertile
principle' that change results from the 'motion, bulk, shape, and
texture of the minute parts of matter.' This was corpuscularianism.
It was the corporeal side of the metaphysics developed earlier on
the continent by René Descartes and, in a different fashion, by
Pierre Gassendi. Boyle's position, prestige, and ceaseless experimentation gave enormous impetus to the development and extension of the corpuscularian, mechanical, anti-Aristotelian world
view.

Along with advocacy of the mechanical world view went advocacy
of the Christian religion. Boyle was a champion of natural theology,
in which properties of the world supported inferences about the
Creator of the world. He advocated the Design Argument. Boyle
at one point said there was incomparably more art expressed in
the structure of a dog's foot than in the famous clock at Strasbourg.[1]
He saw each scientific advance as further glorifying the handiwork
of God. He endowed the Boyle lectures "for proving the Christian
religion against notorious infidels"; he left monies to Harvard University and to William and Mary College for the education of mis-
sionaries.

*The Excellency and Grounds of the Corpuscular or Mechanical Phi-
losophy* (1674), which follows, was originally published as an ap-
pendix to a major theological work, *The Excellency of Theology*. The
former rehearses the advantages of corpuscularianism for chemistry and for science more generally. It deals, as well, with issues
in the methodology of science—the role and status of hypotheses
in science, the degree of certainty they command, and the evalua-
tion of competing scientific claims. These methodological questions
have remained central to philosophy of science. They are part of
the fuzzy border zone between philosophy and science.

---

1. "A disquisition about the final causes of natural things" (1688), in *Works*, T. Birch,
ed., vol. 4, 1744, p. 523. The clock metaphor was widely adduced: Just as the regular
and elaborate Strasbourg clock required a maker, so also did the universe; just as
the workings of the clock were deterministic, so too were the workings of the universe.

See Larry Laudan, "The Clock Metaphor & Hypotheses: The Impact of Descartes on English Methodological Thought, 1650–1670," in his *Science & Hypothesis*,
Dordrecht: Reidel, 1981.

READING

Stewart, M.A., ed. *Selected Philosophical Papers of Robert Boyle*. Manchester: Manchester University Press, 1979.

Boas-Hall, Marie. *Robert Boyle on Natural Philosophy*. Bloomington: Indiana University Press, 1966.

Mandelbaum, M. *Philosophy, Science and Sense Perception*. Baltimore: Johns Hopkins University Press, 1964, ch. 2.

THE EXCELLENCY AND GROUNDS OF THE CORPUSCULAR OR MECHANICAL PHILOSOPHY

By embracing the corpuscular or mechanical philosophy, I am far from supposing with the Epicureans that atoms accidentally meeting in an infinite vacuum were able, of themselves, to produce a world and all its phenomena: nor do I suppose, when God had put into the whole mass of matter an invariable quantity of motion, he needed do no more to make the universe; the material parts being able, by their own unguided motions, to throw themselves into a regular system. The philosophy I plead for reaches but to things purely corporeal; and distinguishing between the first origin of things and the subsequent course of nature, teaches that God indeed gave motion to matter; but that, in the beginning, he so guided the various motion of the parts of it as to contrive them into the world he designed they should compose; and established those rules of motion, and that order amongst things corporeal, which we call the laws of nature. Thus the universe being once framed by God and the laws of motion settled and all upheld by his perpetual concourse and general providence; the same philosophy teaches, that the phenomena of the world are physically produced by the mechancial properties of the parts of matter, and, that they operate upon one another according to mechanical laws. 'Tis of this kind of corpuscular philosophy, that I speak.

And the first thing that recommends it is the intelligibleness or clearness of its principles and explanations. Among the peripatetics[1] there are many intricate disputes about matter, privation, substantial forms, their educations, etc. And the chymists are puzzled to give such definitions, and accounts, of their hypostatical principles[2] as are consistent with one another, and to some obvious phenomena: and much more dark and intricate are their doctrines about the Archeus, Astral Beings, and other odd notions; which perhaps, have in part occasioned the darkness and ambiguity of their expressions, that could not be very clear, when the conceptions were obscure. And if the principles of the Aristotelians and chymists are thus obscure, it is not to be expected that the explications made by the help of such principles only should be intelligible. And, indeed, many of them are so general and slight, or otherwise so unsatisfactory, that, granting their principles, 'tis very hard to understand or admit their applications of them to particular phenomena. And, methinks, even in some of the more ingenious and subtle of the peripatetic discourses, the authors, upon their superficial and narrow theories, have acted more like painters than philosophers; and only shown their skill in making men fancy they see castles, cities, and other structures, that appear solid, magnificent, and extensive; when the whole piece is superficial, artificially made up of colours, and comprized within a frame. But, as to the corpuscular philsophy, men do so easily understand one another's meaning, when they talk of local motion, rest, magnitude, shape, order, situation, and contexture, of material substances; and these principles afford such clear accounts of those things, that are rightly deduced from them alone; that, even such peripatetics or chymists, as maintain other principles, acquiesce in the explications made by these, when they can be had; and seek no further: though, perhaps, the effect be so admirable, as to make it pass for that of a hidden form, or an occult quality. Those very Aristotelians, who believe the celestial bodies to be moved by intelligences, have no recourse to any peculiar agency of theirs to account for eclipses: and we laugh at those East Indians who, to this day, go out in multitudes, with some instruments, to relieve

---

1. Aristotelians, especially the reactionary formalists of the sixteenth and seventeenth centuries.
2. Essential principles or elements. The reference is to the followers of Paracelsus and van Helmont. The "Archeus" is a vital spirit responsible for both chemical and physiological reactions.

the distressed luminary; whose loss of light, they fancy, proceeds from some fainting fit; out of which it must be roused. For no intelligent man, whether chymist or perpatetic, flies to his peculiar principles, after he is informed that the moon is eclipsed, by the interposition of the earth betwixt her, and it; and the sun, by that of the moon, betwixt him and the earth. And, when we see the image of a man cast into the air by a concave spherical speculum; though most men are amazed at it, and some suspect it to be no less than an effect of witchcraft, yet he who is skilled enough in catoptrics will, without consulting Aristotle or Paracelsus or flying to hypostatical principles or substantial forms, be satisfied that the phenomenon is produced by rays of light reflected and made to converge according to optical and mathematical laws.

I next observe that there cannot be fewer principles than the two grand ones of our philosophy, matter and motion; for matter alone, unless it be moved, is wholly unactive; and, whilst all the parts of a body continue in one state, without motion, that body will not exercise any action, or suffer any alteration; though it may, perhaps, modify the action of other bodies that move against it.

Nor can we conceive any principles more primary than matter and motion: for either both of them were immediately created by God; or, if matter be eternal, motion must either be produced by some immaterial supernatural agent; or it must immediately flow, by way of emanation, from the nature of the matter it appertains to.

There cannot be any physical principles more simple than matter and motion; neither of them being resoluble into any other thing.

The next thing which recommends the corpuscular principles is their extensiveness. The genuine and necessary effect of the strong motion of one part of matter against another is either to drive it on, in its entire bulk, or to break and divide it into particles of a determinate motion, figure, size, posture, rest, order or texture. The two first of these, for instance, are each of them capable of numerous varieties: for the figure of a portion of matter may either be one of the five regular geometrical figures, some determinate species of solid figures, or irregular, as the grains of sand, feathers, branches, files etc. And, as the figure, so the motion of one of these particles may be exceedingly diversified, not only by the determination to a particular part of the world but by several other things: as by the almost infinitely different degrees of celerity; by the man-

ner of its progression, with or without rotation, etc. and more yet
by the line wherein it moves; as circular, elliptical, parabolical, hy-
perbolical, spiral, etc. For, as later geometricians have shown that
these curves may be compounded of several motions, that is, described by a body whose motion is mixed, and results from two or
more simple motions; so, how many more curves may be made by
new compositions, and recompositions of motion, is not easy to
determine.

Now, since a single particle of matter, by virtue of only two
mechanical properties that belong to it, may be diversified so many
ways; what a vast number of variations may we suppose capable of
being produced by the compositions, and recompositions of myri-
ads of single invisible corpuscles, that may be contained and con-
creted in one small body; and each of them be endued with more
than two or three of the fertile, universal principles above-
mentioned? And the aggregate of those corpuscles may be further
diversified by the texture resulting from their convention into a
body; which, as so made up, has its own magnitude, shape, pores,
and many capacities of acting and suffering, upon account of the
place it holds among other bodies, in a world constituted like ours:
so that, considering the numerous diversifications that compositions and re-compositions may make of a small number, those who
think the mechanical principles may serve, indeed, to account for
the phenomena of some particular part of natural philosophy, as
statics, the theory of planetary motions etc. but prove unapplicable
to all the phenomena of things corporeal seem to imagine, that by
putting together the letters of the alphabet one may, indeed, make
up all the words to be found in Euclid or Virgil, or in the Latin or
English language, but that they can by no means supply words to
all the books of a great library; much less, to all the languages in
the world.

There are other philosophers, who, oberving the great efficacy
of magnitude, situation, motion, and connection in engines are
willing to allow those mechanical principles a great share in the
operations of bodies of a sensible bulk and manifest mechanism;
and, therefore, to be usefully employed, in accounting for the effects and phenomena of such bodies: though they will not admit
that these principles can be applied to the hidden transactions
among the minute particles of bodies; and, therefore, think it necessary to refer these to what they call nature, substantial forms,

real qualities, and the like unmechanical agents. But this is not necessary: for the mechanical properties of matter are to be found, and the laws of motion take place, not only in the great masses and the middle-sized lumps, but in the smallest fragments of matter: a less portion of it being as much a body as a greater, must as necessarily as the other have its determinate bulk and figure. And whoever views sand through a good microscope will easily perceive that each minute grain has as well its own size and shape as a rock or a mountain. Thus too, when we let fall a large stone, and a pebble, from the top of a high building, they both move comformable to the laws of acceleration, in heavy descending bodies: and the rules of motion are observed, not only in cannon-bullets, but in small shot; and the one strikes down a bird, according to the same laws, as the other batters a wall. And though nature works with much finer materials, and employs more curious contrivances, than art; yet an artist, according to the quantity of the matter he employs, the exigency of the design he undertakes, and the magnitude and shape of the instruments he uses, is able to make pieces of work of the same nature or kind, of extremely different bulks where yet the like art, contrivance, and motion may be observed. Thus a smith who, with a hammer and other large instruments, can, out of masses of iron, forge great bars or wedges to make strong and ponderous chains to secure streets and gates may, with lesser instruments, make smaller nails, and filings, almost as minute as dust; and with yet finer tools, make links wonderfully light and slender. And therefore, to say that though in natural bodies, whose bulk is manifest and their structure visible, the mechanical principles may be usefully admitted but are not to be extended to such portions of matter, whose parts and texture are invisible, is like allowing that the laws of mechanism may take place in a town-clock, and not in a pocket-watch: or, because the terraqueous globe is a vast magnetical body, one should affirm that magnetical laws are not to be expected manifest in a small spherical piece of loadstone; yet experience shows us that, notwithstanding the immense disproportion betwixt these two spheres, the terella[3] as well as the earth, hath its poles, equator, and meridians; and in several other magnetical properties resembles the terrestrial globe.

When, to solve the phenomena of nature, agents are made use

---

3. William Gilbert's spherical loadstone.

of which, though they involve no contradiciton in their notions, as
many think substantial forms and real qualities do, yet are such
that we conceive not how they operate to produce effects; such
agents I mean, as the soul of the world, the universal spirit, the
plastic power etc., the curiosity of an inquisitive person is not satisfied hereby; who seeks not so much to know what is the general
agent that produces a phenomenon, as by what means, and after
what manner, it is produced. Sennertus,[4] and other physicians, tell
us of diseases which proceed from incantation; but sure, it is very
trivial to a sober physician, who comes to visit a patient reported
to be bewitched, to hear only that the strange symptoms he meets
with, and would have an account of, are produced by a witch or
the devil; and he will never be satisfied with so short an answer, if
he can by any means reduce those extravagant symptoms to any
more known and stated diseases; as epilepsies, convulsions, hysteric
fits, etc. and if he cannot, he will confess his knowledge of this
distemper to come far short of what might be expected and attained
in other diseases, wherein he thinks himself bound to search into
the morbific matter; and will not be satisfied, till he can, probably,
deduce from that, and the structure of the human body, and other
concurring physical causes, the phenomena of the malady. And it
would be of little satisfaction to one who desires to understand the
causes of the phenomena in a watch, and how it comes to point at
and strike the hours to be told that a certain watch-maker so con-
trived it: or, to him who would know the true causes of an echo,
to be answered that it is a man, a vault, or a wood, that makes it.

I come now to consider that which I observe most alienates other
sects from the mechanical philosophy; viz. a supposition, that it
pretends to have principles so universal and mathematical that no
other physical hypothesis can be tolerated by it.

This I look upon as an easy, indeed but an important mistake:
for the mechanical principles are so universal, and appliable to so
many purposes, that they are rather fitted to take in, than to ex-
clude, any other hypothesis founded on nature. And such hypotheses, if prudently considered, will be found, as far as they have
truth on their side, to be either legitimately deducible from the

---

4. Daniel Sennert (1572–1637), a widely read German writer on medical and chemical subjects, and an early exponent of a corpuscular chemistry (though he was also
an Aristotelian).

mechanical principles or fairly reconcileable to them. For such hypotheses will, probably, attempt to account for the phenomena of nature, either by the help of a determinate number of material ingredients, such as the tria prima of the chymists,[5] or else by introducing some general agents, as the Platonic soul of the world, and the universal spirit, asserted by some chymists; or, by both these ways together.

Now, the chief thing that a philosopher should look after, in explaining difficult phenomena, is not so much what the agent is or does as, what changes are made in the patient, to bring it to exhibit the phenomena proposed; and by what means, and after what manner, those changes are effected. So that the mechanical philosopher being satisfied, one part of matter can act upon another, only by virtue of local motion, or the effects and consequences thereof; he considers, if the proposed agent be not intelligible and physical, it can never physically explain the phenomena; and if it be intelligible and physical, it will be reducible to matter and some or other of its universal properties. And the indefinite divisibility of matter, the wonderful efficacy of motion, and the almost infinite variety of coalitions and structures that may be made of minute and insensible corpuscles being duly weighed; why may not a philosopher think it possible to make out, by their help, the mechanical possibility of any corporeal agent, how subtle, diffused, or active soever, that can be solidly proved to have a real existence in nature? Though the Cartesians are mechanical philosophers, yet their subtle matter, which the very name declares to be a corporeal substance, is, for ought I know, little less diffused through the universe, or less active in it, than the universal spirit of some chymists; not to say the world soul of the Platonists. But whatever be the physical agent, whether it be inanimate, or living, purely corporeal, or united to an intellectual substance; the above-mentioned changes, wrought in the body made to exhibit the phenomena, may be effected by the same, or the like means; or after the same, or the like manner: as, for instance, if corn be reduced to meal, the materials and shape of the mill-stones and their peculiar motion and adaptation will be much of the same kind; and, to be sure, the grains of corn will suffer a various attrition, and comminution in their passage to the form of meal, whether the

---

5. The Paracelsan elements of salt, sulphur, and mercury.

corn be ground by a watermill, or a windmill, a horsemill, or a handmill; that is, a mill, whose stones are turned by inanimate, by brute, or by rational agents. And if an angel himself should work a real change in the nature of a body, 'tis scarce conceivable to men how he could do it without the assistance of local motion; since, if nothing were displaced, or otherwise moved than before it is hardly conceivable how it should be, in itself, different from what it was before.

But if the chymists, or others, who would deduce a compleat natural philosophy from salt, sulphur, and mercury, or any determined number of ingredients of things, would well consider what they undertake, they might easily discover that the material parts of bodies can reach but to a few phenomena of nature, whilst these things [ingredients] are considered but as quiescent things, whence, they would find themselves to suppose them active; and that things purely corporeal cannot but by means of local motion, and the effects that may result from it, be very variously shaped, sized, and combined parts of matter: so that the chymists must leave the greatest part of the phenomena of the universe unexplained, by means of the ingredients of bodies, without taking in the mechanical and more comprehensive properties of matter, especially local motion. I willingly grant that salt, sulphur, and mercury, or some substances analogous to them, are obtainable, by the action of the fire, from a very great many dissipable bodies here below. Nor do I deny that in explaining several phenomena of such bodies, it may be of use to a naturalist to know and consider that as sulphur, for instance, abounds in the body proposed, it may be, thence, probably argued that the qualities usually attending that principle, when predominant, may be also upon its account found in the body that so largely partakes of it. But, though chymical explications are, sometimes, the most obvious, yet they are not the most fundamental and satisfactory: for the chymical ingredient itself, whether sulphur, or any other must owe its nature and other qualities to the union of insensible particles, in a convenient size, shape, motion, or rest, and texture; all which are but mechanical properties of convening corpuscles. And this may be illustrated by what happens in artificial fire-works. For, though in most of those sorts, made either for war, or recreation, gun-powder be a principal ingredient; and many of the phenomena may be derived from the greater or less proportion wherein it enters the compositions: yet there may be fire-works made without gun-powder, as appears by those of the ancient Greeks and Romans. And gun-powder owes its aptness to fire, and to be exploded, to the mechanical texture of more simple portions of matter, nitre, charcoal, and sulphur. And sulphur itself, though it be by many chymists mistaken for an hypostatical [essential] principle, owes its inflammability to the union of still more simple and primary corpuscles; since chymists confess that it had an inflammable ingredient: and experience shows that it very much abounds with an acid and uninflammable salt and is not destitute of a terrestrial part. It may, indeed, be here alleged that the productions of chymical analyses are simple bodies; and, upon that account, irresoluble; but that several substances, which chymists call the salts, sulphurs, or mercuries of the bodies that afford them, are not simple and homogeneous is demonstrable. Nor is their not being easily dissipable, or resoluble, a clear proof of their not being made up of more primitive portions of matter. For compounded bodies may be as difficultly resoluble as most of those that chymists obtain by the fire: witness common greenglass, which is far more durable, and irresoluble, than many of those which pass for hypostatical substances. And some enamels will, for everal times, even vitrify in the forge, without losing their nature or often so much as their colour: yet, enamel consists of salt, powder of pebbles, or sand, and calcined tin; and, if not white, usually of some tinging metal or mineral. But how indestructible soever the chymical principles are supposed, several of the operations ascribed to them will never be made appear without the help of local motion: were it not for this, we can but little better solve the phenomena of many bodies by knowing what ingredients compose them than we can explain the operations of a watch by knowing of how many and of what metals, the balance, the wheels, the chain, and other parts consist; or than we can derive the operations of a windmill from barely knowing that it is made up of wood, stone, canvas, and iron. And here let me add that it would not at all overthrow the corpuscularian hypothesis, though, either by more exquisite purifications or by some other operations, than the usual analysis by fire, it should appear that the material principles of mixed bodies are not the tria prima of the vulgar chymists; but, either substances of another nature, or fewer in number; or, if it were true that the Helmontians had such a resolving menstruum as their master's alkahest,[6] by which he affirms that he could reduce stones into salt, of the same weight with the mineral; and bring both that salt, and all other mixed and tangible bodies, into insipid water. For whatever be the number or qualities of the chymical principles, if they really exist in nature, it may very possibly be shown that they are made up of insensible corpuscles, of determinate bulks and shapes: and, by the various coalitions and textures of such corpuscles, many material ingredients may be composed, or made to result. But though the alkahestical reductions, newly mentioned, should be admitted, yet the mechanical principles might well be accommodated even to them. For the solidity, taste, etc. of salt may be fairly accounted for by the stiffness, sharpness, and other mechanical properties of the minute particles whereof salt consists: and if, by a farther action of the alkahest, the salt, or any other solid body, be reduced into insipid water, this also may be explained by the same principles; supposing a farther comminution of its parts, and such an attrition as wears off the edges and points that enabled them to strike briskly upon the organ of taste: for as to fluidity and firmness, they, principally, depend upon two of our grand principles, motion and rest. And 'tis certain that the agitation, or rest, and the looser contact, or closer cohesion of the particles, is able to make the same portion of matter at one time a firm and at another a fluid body. So that, though future sagacity and industry of chymists should obtain, from mixed bodies, homogeneous substances, different in number, nature, or both, from their vulgar salt, sulphur, and mercury; yet the corpuscular philosophy is so general and fertile as to be fairly reconcilable to such a discovery; and also so useful, that these new material principles will, as well as the old tria prima, stand in need of the more universal principles of the corpuscularians; especially of local motion. And, indeed, whatever elements or ingredients men have pitched upon; yet, if they take not in the mechanical properties of matter, their principles are so deficient that I have observed both the materialists and chymists not only leave many things unexplained, to which their narrow principles will not extend; but, even in the particulars they presume to give an account of, they either content themselves to assign such common and indefinite causes as are too general to be satisfactory; or, if they ven-

---

6. A universal solvent.

ture to give particular causes, they assign precarious or false ones, liable to be easily disproved by circumstances, or instances, whereto their doctrines will not agree. The chymists, however, need not be frightened from acknowledging the prerogative of the mechanical philosophy, since that may be reconcilable with the truth of their own principles, so far as they agree with the phenomena they are applied to: for these more confined hypotheses may be subordinate to those more general and fertile principles; and there can be no ingredient assigned that has a real existence in nature but may be derived, either immediately or by a row of compositions, from the universal matter, modified by its mechanical properties. For if with the same bricks, differently put together and ranged, several bridges, vaults, houses, and other structures may be raised merely by a various contrivance of parts of the same kind; what a great variety of ingredients may be produced by nature from the various coalitions and contextures of corpuscles, that need not be supposed, like bricks, all of the same size and shape; but to have, both in the one and the other, as great a variety as could be wished for? And the primary and minute concretions that belong to these ingredients may, without opposition from the mechanical philosophy, be supposed to have their particles so minute and strongly coherent that nature of herself scarce ever tears them asunder. Thus mercury and gold may be successively made to put on a multitude of disguises; and yet so retain their nature as to be reducible to their pristine forms.

From hence it is probable if, besides rational souls, there be any immaterial substances, such as the heavenly intelligences, and the substantial forms of the Aristotelians, that are regularly to be numbered among natural agents; their way of working being unknown to us, they can only help to constitute and effect things, but will very little help us to conceive how things are effects; so that, by whatever principles natural things are constituted, 'tis by the mechanical principles that their phenomena must be clearly explained. For instance though we grant, with the Aristotelians, that the planets are made of a quintessential matter and moved by angels or immaterial intelligences; yet, to explain the stations, progressions and retrogradations, and other phenomena of the planets, we must have recourse either to excentrics, epicycles, etc. or to motions, made in elliptical, or other peculiar lines; and, in a word, to theories wherein the motion, figure, situation and other mathematical, or mechanical properties are chiefly employed. But if the principles proposed be corporeal, they will then be fairly reducible or reconcilable to the mechanical principles; these being so general and fertile that, among real material things, there is none but may be derived from or reduced to them. And when the chymists shall show that mixed bodies owe their qualities to the predominance of any one of their three grand ingredients, the corpuscularians will show that the very qualities of this or that ingredient flow from its peculiar texture, and the mechanical properties of the corpuscles that compose it. And to affirm that because the chemical furnaces afford a great number of uncommon productions, and phenomena, that there are bodies or operations amongst things purely corporeal not derivable from or reconcilable to the principles of mechanical philosophy is to say, because there are many and various hymns, pavanes, threnodies, courants, gavottes, sarabands, etc. in a music book, many of the tunes, or notes have no dependence on the scale of music; or as if because excepting rhomboids, squares, pentagons, chiliagons, and numerous other polygons, one should affirm there are some rectilineal figures not reducible to triangles, or that have properties which overthrow Euclid's doctrine of triangles and polygons.

I shall only add that as mechanical principles and explanations, where they can be had, are, for their clearness, preferred by materialists themselves; so the sagacity and industry of modern naturalists and mathematicians, having happily applied them to several of those difficult phenomena which before were referred to occult qualities it is probable that when this philosophy is more scrutinized and farther improved, it will be found applicable to the solution of still more phenomena of nature. And 'tis not always necessary that he who advances an hypothesis in astronomy, chymistry, anatomy, etc. be able, a priori, to prove it true, or demonstratively to show that the other hypothesis proposed about the same subject must be false; for as Plato said that the world is God's epistle to mankind; and might have added, in his own way, that it was written in mathematical characters; so, in the physical explanations of the parts of the system of the world, methinks there is somewhat like what happens when men conjecturally frame several keys to read a letter written in ciphers. For though one man, by his sagacity, finds the right key, it will be very difficult for him either to prove, otherwise than by trial, that any particular word is not such as 'tis guessed to be by others, according to their keys; or to show, a priori, that theirs are to be rejected and his to be preferred; yet, if due trial being made, the key he proposes be found so agreeable to the characters of the letter, as to enable one to understand them, and make coherent sense of them, its suitableness to what it should decipher is, without either confutations or foreign positive proofs, alone sufficient to make it accepted as the right key of that cipher. Thus, in physical hypotheses, there are some that, without falling foul upon others, peaceably obtain the approbation of discerning men only by their fitness to solve the phenomena for which they were devised, without thwarting any known observation or law of nature; and therefore, if the mechanical philosophy shall continue to explain corporeal things, as it has of late, 'tis scarce to be doubted but that in time unprejudiced persons will think it sufficiently recommended, by its being consistent with itself and applicable to so many phenomena of nature.

Huygens

Treatise on Light (1678)   Preface (the hypothetico-
deductive method)

Chapter 1 (an argument with
Descartes)

Christian Huygens was born in 1629 into a Dutch family of scholars
and diplomats. He early developed skills and interests in mathematics and manual arts. At seventeen he entered into philosophical
and scientific correspondence with Mersenne and Descartes. By his
mid-twenties he was the foremost lens grinder in Europe, he had
discovered a satellite of Saturn, and he had invented the pendulum
clock by correcting Galileo's inaccurate claim that ordinary pendulums were isochronic. In the period between Descartes and Leibniz, he was justly acclaimed as Europe's greatest mathematician.
He was a founding member of both the English *Royal Society* (1663)
and the French *Académie Royale des Sciences* (1666). He made orginal
and lasting contributions to optics, mechanics, geometry, hydro-
statics, and astronomy. He died in 1695.

Although remembered as a scientist (his wave theory of light is
familiar to most neophyte physics students), Huygens's work was
infused with philosophical concerns: it was in the tradition of natural philosophy. He dealt with issues in ontology, epistemology,
methodology, and theology. Although differing from Descartes in
some respects, he developed the Cartesian programme of explaining all phenomena—gravitational, magnetic, optical, electric, and
chemical—from the "two catholic principles" of matter and motion.
In this he had no equal in the seventeenth century.

In Huygens's time, the telescope and microscope played major
roles in the arbitration of scientific disputes and of borderline philosophical disputes, such as the possibility of living things being gen-

erated from nonliving. Because both instruments depended on the transmission and amplification of light, it was natural that the nature and properties of light should be the subject of earnest inquiry. As a mathematician and optical-instrument maker, Huygens was ideally suited to advance these inquiries.

His *Treatise on Light* was written in 1678 and published in 1690. Its full title continues: 'in which is explained the causes of that which occurs in reflexion and in refraction and particularly in the strange refraction of Iceland Crystal.' The 'strange refraction' was the just-discovered property of polarisation. He explains this and other optical phenomena by the principles of the 'true philosophy, in which one conceives the causes of all natural effects in terms of mechanical motions.' For Huygens, philosophical theories about the nature and constitution of the world were subject to scientific and experimental testing. Again, what at one time is philosophical, speculative, and programmatic becomes at a later time scientific, if the research based on the 'philosophy' is fruitful.

The preface of his *Treatise* contains one of the earliest and clearest statements of the hypothetical-deductive method in science. It occurs in the context of contrasting the probabilism of science with the certainty of geometry. Although often not recognised, this was the view of Descartes, for whom the hypotheses of science were at best only highly probable.

READING

Thompson, Silvanus P., ed. *Huygens: Treatise on Light.* Chicago: University of Chicago Press, 1945.

Bell, E.A. *Christian Huygens and the Development of Science in the Seventeenth Century.* London: E. Arnold, 1947.

Bos, H.J.M., et al., eds. *Studies on Christian Huygens.* Lisse: Swets & Zeitlinger B.V., 1980.

TREATISE ON LIGHT

PREFACE

This treatise was written during my stay in Paris twelve years ago, and in the year 1678 was presented to the Royal Academy of Sciences, to which the king had been pleased to call me. Several of this body who are still living, especially those who have devoted themselves to the study of mathematics, will remember having been at the meeting at which I presented the paper; of these I recall only those distinguished gentlemen Messrs. Cassini, Römer, and De la Hire. Although since then I have corrected and changed several passages, the copies which I had made at that time will show that I have added nothing except some conjectures concerning the structure of Iceland spar and an additional remark concerning refraction in rock-crystal. I mention these details to show how long I have been thinking about these matters which I am only just now publishing, and not at all to detract from the merit of those who, without having seen what I have written, may have investigated similar subjects: as, indeed, happened in the case of two distinguished mathematicians, Newton and Leibniz, regarding the question of the proper figure for a converging lens, one surface being given.

It may be asked why I have so long delayed the publication of this work. The reason is that I wrote it rather carelessly in French, expecting to translate it into Latin, and, in the meantime, to give the subject still further attention. Later I thought of publishing this volume together with another on dioptrics in which I discuss the theory of the telescope and the phenomena associated with it. But soon the subject was no longer new and was therefore less interesting. Accordingly I kept putting off the work from time to time, and now I do not know when I shall be able to finish it, for my time is largely occupied either by business or by some new investigation.

In view of these facts I have thought wise to publish this manuscript in its present state rather than to wait longer and run the risk of its being lost.

One finds in this subject a kind of demonstration which does not carry with it so high a degree of certainty as that employed in geometry; and which differs distinctly from the method employed by geometers in that they prove their propositions by well-established and incontrovertible principles, while here principles are tested by the inferences which are derivable from them. The nature of the subject permits of no other treatment. It is possible, however, in this way to establish a probability which is little short of certainty. This is the case when the consequences of the assumed principles are in perfect accord with the observed phenomena, and especially when these verifications are numerous; but above all when one employs the hypothesis to predict new phenomena and finds his expectations realized.

If in the following treatise all these evidences of probability are present, as, it seems to me, they are, the correctness of my conclusions will be confirmed; and, indeed, it is scarcely possible that these matters differ very widely from the picture which I have drawn of them. I venture to hope that those who enjoy finding out causes and who appreciate the wonders of light will be interested in these various speculations and in the new explanation of that remarkable property upon which the structure of the human eye depends and upon which are based those instruments which so powerfully aid the eye. I trust also there will be some who, from such beginnings, will push these investigations far in advance of what I have been able to do; for the subject is not one which is easily exhausted. This will be evident especially from those parts of the subject which I have indicated as too difficult for solution; and still more evident from those matters upon which I have not touched at all, such as the various kinds of luminous bodies and the whole question of color, which no one can yet boast of having explained.

Finally, there is much more to be learned by investigation concerning the nature of light than I have yet discovered; and I shall be greatly indebted to those who, in the future, shall furnish what is needed to complete my imperfect knowledge.

The Hague, 8th of January, 1690.

CHAPTER I

On the Rectilinear Propagation of Rays

Demonstrations in optics, as in every science where geometry is applied to matter, are based upon experimental facts; as, for instance, that light travels in straight lines, that the angles of incidence and reflection are equal, and that rays of light are refracted according to the law of sines. For this last fact is now as widely known and as certainly known as either of the preceding.

Most writers upon optical subjects have been satisfied to assume these facts. But others, of a more investigating turn of mind, have tried to find the origin and the cause of these facts, considering them in themselves interesting natural phenomena. And although they have advanced some ingenious ideas, these are not such that the more intelligent readers do not still want further explanation in order to be thoroughly satisfied.

Accordingly, I here submit some considerations on this subject with the hope of elucidating, as best I may, this department of natural science, which not undeservedly has gained the reputation of being exceedingly difficult. I feel myself especially indebted to those who first began to make clear these deeply obscure matters, and to lead us to hope that they were capable of simple explanations.

But, on the other hand, I have been astonished to find these same writers accepting arguments which are far from evident as if they were conclusive and demonstrative. No one has yet given even a probable explanation of the fundamental and remarkable phenomena of light, *viz.* why it travels in straight lines and how rays coming from an infinitude of different directions cross one another without disturbing one another.

I shall attempt, in this volume, to present in accordance with the principles of modern philosophy, some clearer and more probable reasons, first, for the rectilinear propagation of light, and secondly, for its reflection when it meets other bodies. Later I shall explain the phenomenon of rays which are said to undergo refraction in passing through transparent bodies of different kinds. Here I shall treat also of refraction effects due to the varying density of the earth's atmosphere. Afterwards I shall examine the causes of that peculiar refraction occurring in a certain crystal which comes from Iceland. And lastly, I shall consider the different shapes required in transparent and in reflecting bodies to converge rays upon a single point or to deflect them in various ways. Here we shall see with what ease are determined, by our new theory, not only the ellipses, hyperbolas, and other curves which M. Descartes has so ingeniously devised for this purpose, but also the curve which one surface of a lens must have when the other surface is given, as spherical, plane, or of any figure whatever.

We cannot help believing that light consists in the motion of a certain material. For when we consider its production we find that here on the earth it is generally produced by fire and flame which, beyond doubt, contain bodies in a state of rapid motion, since they are able to dissolve and melt numerous other more solid bodies.

And if we consider its effects, we see that when light is converged, as, for instance, by concave mirrors, it is able to produce combustion just as fire does; i.e., it is able to tear bodies apart; a property that surely indicates motion, at least in the true philosophy where one believes all natural phenomena to be mechanical effects. And, in my opinion, we must admit this, or else give up all hope of ever understanding anything in physics.

Since, according to this philosophy, it is considered certain that the sensation of sight is caused only by the impulse of some form of matter upon the nerves at the base of the eye, we have here still another reason for thinking that light consists in a motion of the matter situated between us and the luminous body.

When we consider, further, the very great speed with which light is propagated in all directions, and the fact that when rays come from different directions, even those directly opposite, they cross without disturbing each other, it must be evident that we do not see luminous objects by means of matter translated from the object to us, as a shot or an arrow travels through the air. For certainly this would be in contradiction to the two properties of light which we have just mentioned, and especially to the latter. Light is then propagated in some other manner, an understanding of which we may obtain from our knowledge of the manner in which sound travels through the air.

We know that through the medium of the air, an invisible and impalpable body, sound is propagated in all directions, from the point where it is produced, by means of a motion which is communicated successively from one part of the air to another; and since this motion travels with the same speed in all directions, it must form spherical surfaces which continually enlarge until finally they strike our ear. Now there can be no doubt that light also comes from the luminous body to us by means of some motion impressed upon the matter which lies in the intervening space; for we have already seen that this cannot occur through the translation of matter from one point to the other.

If, in addition, light requires time for its passage—a point we shall presently consider—it will then follow that this motion is impressed upon the matter gradually, and hence is propagated, as that of sound, by surfaces and spherical waves. I call these *waves* because of their resemblance to those which are formed when one

throws a pebble into water and which represent gradual propagation in circles, although produced by a different cause and confined to a plane surface.

As to the question of light requiring time for its propagation, let
us consider first whether there is any experimental evidence to the
contrary.

What we can do here on the earth with sources of light placed
at great distances (although showing that light does not occupy a
sensible time in passing over these distances) may be objected to
on the ground that these distances are still too small, and that,
therefore, we can conclude only that the propagation of light is
exceedingly rapid. M. Descartes thought it instantaneous, and
based his opinion upon much better evidence, furnished by the
eclipse of the moon. Nevertheless, as I shall show, even this evidence
is not conclusive. I shall state the matter in a manner slightly different from his in order that we may more easily arrive at all the
consequences.

Let A be the position of the sun; BD a part of the orbit or annual
path of the earth; ABC a straight line intersecting in C the orbit
of the moon, which is represented by the circle CD.

If, now, light requires time—say one hour—to traverse the space
between the earth and the moon, it follows that when the earth has
reached the point B, its shadow, or the interruption of light, will
not yet have reached the point C, and will not reach it until one
hour later. Counting from the time when the earth occupies the
position B, it will be one hour later that the moon arrives at the
point C and is there obscured; but this eclipse or interruption of
light will not be visible at the earth until the end of still another
hour. Let us suppose that during these two hours the earth has
moved to the position E. From this point the moon will appear to

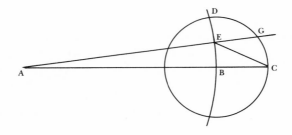

be eclipsed at C, a position which it occupied one hour before, while the sun will be seen at A. For I assume with Copernicus that the sun is fixed and, since light travels in straight lines, must always be seen it its true position. But it is a matter of universal observation, we are told, that the eclipsed moon appears in that part of the ecliptic directly opposite the sun; while according to our view its position ought to be behind this by the angle GEC, the supplement of the angle AEC. But this is contrary to the fact, for the angle GEC will be quite easily observed, amounting to about 33°. Now according to our computation, which will be found in the memoir on the causes of the phenomena of Saturn, the distance, BA, between the earth and the sun is about 12,000 times the diameter of the earth, and consequently 400 times the distance of the moon, which is 30 diameters. The angle ECB will, therefore, be almost 400 times as great as BAE, which is 5′ $viz.$, the angular distance traversed by the earth in its orbit during an interval of two hours. Thus the angle BCE amounts to almost 33°, and likewise the angle CEG, which is 5′ greater.

But it must be noted that in this argument the speed of light is assumed to be such that the time required for it to pass from here to the moon is one hour. If, however, we suppose that it requires only a minute of time, then evidently the angle CEG will amount to only 33′; and if it requires only ten seconds of time, this angle will amount to less than 6′. But so small a quantity is not easily observed in a lunar eclipse, and consequently it is not allowable to infer the instantaneous propagation of light.

It is somewhat unusual, we must confess, to assume a speed one hundred thousand times as great as that of sound, which, according to my observations, travels about 180 toises [1151 *feet*] in a second, or during a pulse-beat; but this supposition appears by no means impossible, for it is not a question of carrying a body with such speed, but of a motion passing successively from one point to another.

I do not therefore, in thinking of these matters, hesitate to suppose that the propagation of light occupies time, for on this view all the phenomena can be explained, while on the contrary view none of them can be explained. Indeed, it seems to me, and to many others also, that M. Descartes, whose object has been to discuss all physical subjects in a clear way, and who has certainly succeeded better than any one before him, has written nothing on light and its properties which is not either full of difficulty or even inconceivable.

But this idea which I have advanced only as a hypothesis has recently been almost established as a fact by the ingenious method of Römer, whose work I propose here to describe, expecting that he himself will later give a complete confirmation of this view.

NEWTON

Principia (1687)	Preface to First Edition (mathematical and scientific methods)
	Scholium (on absolute space and time) Rules of Reasoning in Philosophy General Scholium (design argument, hypotheses in science)
Opticks (1704)	Query 31 (nature, corpuscularianism, gravity, the design argument, hypotheses in science)

Isaac Newton was the towering intellect of the Scientific Revolution. In a period blessed with so many outstanding thinkers, he was simply the most outstanding. Goethe labeled 1642, the year of Newton's birth, the "Christmas of the modern age." Newton made fundamental contributions in many fields—mechanics, optics, astronomy, mathematics, chemistry—and any one of these would have assured him an honoured place in the history of science. Additionally he wrote one and a third million words on theological and biblical issues and over half a million on alchemy. Indeed, Newton wrote much more on these topics than he did on science. He was a member of Parliament, longtime President of the Royal Society, and Master of the British Mint. He died in 1727 and was buried in Westminster Abbey.

Newton corresponded and argued with all the prominent philosophers of his age: Boyle, Robert Hooke, Huygens, Henry More, Bishop George Berkeley, John Wallis, John Locke, and G.W. Leibniz. Both the debates with Leibniz over the possibility of absolute space and time and the consequence thereof for science, religion, and cognition and his debates with Cartesians concerning how gravitational attraction could be reconciled with a mechanical world view illustrate the then-acknowledged interaction of physics and metaphysics.

Newton's influence on the history of science is unequaled, but his influence extended well beyond science. His achievements became a standard for intellectual effort in all fields. Newton had himself indicated the path: 'If natural Philosophy in all its Parts, by pursuing this Method, shall at length be perfected, the Bounds of Moral Philosophy will be also enlarged.'[1] David Hume in the preface to his *Treatise* claimed he is following Newton's path. Immanuel Kant based the philosophy of his *Critique of Pure Reason* partly upon the assumption that Newton had discovered the correct system of the world. He says at one point that the 'true method of metaphysics is basically the same as that introduced by Newton into natural science and which had such useful consequences in that field.'[2] A great many theologians, moralists, economists, and chemists tried to emulate Newton. The more general enthusiasm for Newton was captured in Pope's epitaph:

> Nature and Nature's laws lay hid in night:
> God said, Let Newton be! and all was light.

Newton's *magnum opus* is his *Principia*,[3] published in 1687. Its full title is *The Mathematical Principles of Natural Philosophy*. A clue to the method of this epochal work is contained in a piece originally meant as its preface but not published till it occurred as Query 31 in the second edition of the *Opticks* (1717). He says:

> As in Mathematics, so in Natural Philosophy, the Investigation of difficult things by the Method of Analysis ought ever to precede the Method of Composition.[4]

---

1. Isaac Newton, *Opticks*, New York: Dover, 1952, p. 405.
2. Kant, *Selected Precritical Writings and Correspondence with Beck*, G.K. Kenford and D.E. Walford, trans., Manchester: Manchester University Press, 1968, p. 17.
3. Florian Cajori, trans., Berkeley: University of California Press, 1934.
4. *Opticks*, New York: Dover, 1979, p. 404. On the method of analysis and synthesis in geometry, see J. Hintikka and U. Remes, *The Method of Analysis: Its Geometrical Origin and Its General Significance*, Boston: Reidel, 1974.

Mathematics and physics have similar methods. This is of course a most un-Aristotelian position: the separation of mathematics and physics greatly limited medieval science.[5]

A further clue to the method of the *Principia* occurs in the published preface to the first edition. In talking of the difference between geometrical objects (the perfect figures of Euclid and Pythagoras) and the material objects made by artisans, he follows Galileo in saying, 'errors are not in the art but in the artificers.' If technology and craft could produce a perfect sphere, its properties would be exactly as the mathematicians tell us. More generally Newton sees the scientific experiment as attempts at or approximations to the objectification of scientific theory. The scientist does not merely look at undisturbed nature in the Aristotelian manner: The experiment is an attempt to create a part of nature in the image of the theory, to objectify the theory.[6] Newton's procedure is that of idealization. He deals with the mathematics of ideal and abstracted situations *before* he considers the properties of real objects. This is the reverse of Aristotelian naturalism. The structure of the *Principia* displays the procedure. The first four hundred pages are entirely mathematical and deal with clearly idealised situations: a body considered as a point moving in a circle, pendulums moving in voids, two-body universes, etc. It is not until the third and final book that he considers how actual bodies move in the world around us.

It is a matter of some moment whether Newton's empiricist supporters—Locke, Hume, Mill, et al.—grasped the method of the *Principia*. With good reason, many think that they did not.[7]

Newton's second major work was his *Opticks* of 1704. This presents in marvelous sweep and detail his experimental genius. Consistent with the mechanical world view, he developed a corpuscular, or particle, theory of light. In a second edition of 1717, he added a lengthy series of reflections of a philosophical and methodological kind dealing with gravity, the theory of matter, the Design Argu-

---

5. The matter is not entirely clear-cut. See James G. Lennox, "Aristotle, Galileo, and 'Mixed Sciences'," in William A. Wallace, ed., *Reinterpreting Galileo*, Washington: Catholic University of America Press, 1986, pp. 29–51.
6. See Gaston Bachelard, *The New Scientific Spirit* (1934), Boston: Beacon Press, 1984.
7. Jürgen Mittelstrass, "The Galilean Revolution: The Historical Fate of a Methodological Insight," *Studies in the History and Philosophy of Science*, 1972, 2(4), 297–328.

ment, the role of hypotheses in natural philosophy, and other topics.

Newton saw his work as advancing the tradition of natural theology. He said he wrote the *Principia* with 'an eye upon such principles as might work with considering men for the belief of a Deity.'[8] And in endorsing the Design Argument, he said that discourse about God 'from the appearances of things, does certainly belong to Natural Philosophy'.[9] The arguments that raged with his opponents on the continent demonstrates the intertwining of physics, philosophy, and theology so characteristic not just of Newton but of all natural philosophy of the Scientific Revolution. In rejecting Newton's claim that the amount of motion in the world is steadily decreasing, Leibniz said that it requires that 'God Almighty wants to wind up his watch (the universe) from time to time: otherwise it would cease to move.'[10] To understand this debate, so crucial to the emergence of the 'scientific' idea of the conservation of energy, requires appreciation of science, theology, and philosophy.

A further example of these interconnections was Newton's grand unifying theory of gravitation. This monumental achievement combined Kepler's laws for planetary motion and Galileo's law of falling bodies into the single inverse-square law of gravitational attraction. Yet it was immediately attacked by Leibniz and Cartesian physicists as being occult, as turning the clock back to Aristotelian physics. The idea of attraction at a distance, without any intermediary mechanism, was seen as incompatible with the hard-won, new, mechanical world view. The understanding of gravitation remains at the interface of science and philosophy.

READING

Cohen, I. Bernard. *The Newtonian Revolution.* Cambridge: Cambridge University Press, 1980.

Manuel, Frank E. *A Portrait of Isaac Newton.* Cambridge, Mass.: Harvard University Press, 1968.

---

8. H.S. Thayer, ed., *Newton's Philosophy of Nature*, New York: Hafner, 1953, p 46.
9. *Principia*, p. 546.
10. H.G. Alexander, ed., *The Leibniz-Clarke Correspondence*, New York: Barnes and Noble, 1956, p. 11.

Westfall, Richard S. *Never at Rest: A Biography of Isaac Newton.* Cambridge: Cambridge University Press, 1980.

PRINCIPIA

NEWTON'S PREFACE TO THE FIRST EDITION

Since the ancients (as we are told by *Pappus*) esteemed the science of mechanics of greatest importance in the investigation of natural things, and the moderns, rejecting substantial forms and occult qualities, have endeavored to subject the phenomena of nature to the laws of mathematics, I have in this treatise cultivated mathematics as far as it related to philosophy. The ancients considered mechanics in a twofold respect; as rational, which proceeds accurately by demonstration, and practical. To practical mechanics all the manual arts belong, from which mechanics took its name. But as artificers do not work with perfect accuracy, it comes to pass that mechanics is so distinguished from geometry that what is perfectly accurate is called geometrical; what is less so, is called mechanical. However, the errors are not in the art, but in the artificers. He that works with less accuracy is an imperfect mechanic; and if any could work with perfect accuracy, he would be the most perfect mechanic of all, for the description of right lines and circles, upon which geometry is founded, belongs to mechanics. Geometry does not teach us to draw these lines, but requires them to be drawn, for it requires that the learner should first be taught to describe these accurately before he enters upon geometry, then it shows how by these operations problems may be solved. To describe right lines and circles are problems, but not geometrical problems. The solution of these problems is required from mechanics, and by geometry the use of them, when so solved, is shown; and it is the glory of geometry that from those few principles, brought from without, it is able to produce so many things. Therefore geometry is founded in mechanical practice, and is nothing but that part of universal mechanics which accurately proposes and demonstrates the art of measuring. But since the manual arts are chiefly employed in the moving of bodies, it happens that geometry is commonly referred to their magnitude, and mechanics to their motion. In this sense rational mechanics will be the science of motions resulting from any forces whatsoever, and of the forces required to produce any motions, accurately proposed and demonstrated. This part of mechanics, as far as it extended to the five powers which relate to manual arts, was cultivated by the ancients, who considered gravity (it not being a manual power) no otherwise than in moving weights by those powers. But I consider philosophy rather than arts and write not concerning manual but natural powers, and consider chiefly those things which relate to gravity, levity, elastic force, the resistance of fluids, and the like forces, whether attractive or impulsive; and therefore I offer this work as the mathematical principles of philosophy, for the whole burden of philosophy seems to consist in this—from the phenomena of motions to investigate the forces of nature, and then from these forces to demonstrate the other phenomena; and to this end the general propositions in the first and second Books are directed. In the third Book I give an example of this in the explication of the System of the World; for by the propositions mathematically demonstrated in the former Books, in the third I derive from the celestial phenomena the forces of gravity with which bodies tend to the sun and the several planets. Then from these forces, by other propositions which are also mathematical, I deduce the motions of the planets, the comets, the moon, and the sea. I wish we could derive the rest of the phenomena of Nature by the same kind of reasoning from mechanical principles, for I am induced by many reasons to suspect that they may all depend upon certain forces by which the particles of bodies, by some causes hitherto unknown, are either mutually impelled towards one another, and cohere in regular figures, or are repelled and recede from one another. These forces being unknown, philosophers have hitherto attempted the search of Nature in vain; but I hope the principles here laid down will afford some light either to this or some truer method of philosophy.

In the publication of this work the most acute and universally learned Mr. *Edmund Halley* not only assisted me in correcting the errors of the press and preparing the geometrical figures, but it was through his solicitations that it came to be published; for when he had obtained of me my demonstrations of the figure of the celestial orbits, he continually pressed me to communicate the same to the *Royal Society*, who afterwards, by their kind encouragement and entreaties, engaged me to think of publishing them. But after I had begun to consider the inequalities of the lunar motions, and had entered upon some other things relating to the laws and measures of gravity and other forces; and the figures that would be described by bodies attracted according to given laws; and the motion of several bodies moving among themselves; the motion of bodies in resisting mediums; the forces, densities, and motions, of mediums; the orbits of the comets, and such like, I deferred that publication till I had made a search into those matters, and could put forth the whole together. What relates to the lunar motions (being imperfect), I have put all together in the corollaries of Prop. LXVI, to avoid being obliged to propose and distinctly demonstrate the several things there contained in a method more prolix than the subject deserved and interrupt the series of the other propositions. Some things, found out after the rest, I chose to insert in places less suitable, rather than change the number of the propositions and the citations. I heartily beg that what I have here done may be read with forbearance; and that my labors in a subject so difficult may be examined, not so much with the view to censure, as to remedy their defects.

Is. Newton

Cambridge, Trinity College, May 8, 1686.

Scholium on Absolute Space and Time

Hitherto I have laid down the definitions of such words as are less known, and explained the sense in which I would have them to be understood in the following discourse. I do not define time, space, place, and motion, as being well known to all. Only I must observe, that the common people conceive those quantities under no other notions but from the relation they bear to sensible objects. And thence arise certain prejudices, for the removing of which it will be convenient to distinguish them into absolute and relative, true and apparent, mathematical and common.

I. Absolute, true, and mathematical time, of itself, and from its own nature, flows equably without relation to anything external, and by another name is called duration: relative, apparent, and common time, is some sensible and external (whether accurate or unequable) measure of duration by the means of motion, which is commonly used instead of true time; such as an hour, a day, a month, a year.

II. Absolute space, in its own nature, without relation to anything external, remains always similar and immovable. Relative space is some movable dimension or measure of the absolute spaces; which our senses determine by its position to bodies; and which is commonly taken for immovable space; such is the dimension of a subterraneous, an aerial, or celestial space, determined by its position in respect of the earth. Absolute and relative space are the same in figure and magnitude; but they do not remain always numerically the same. For if the earth, for instance, moves, a space of our air, which relatively and in respect of the earth remains always the same, will at one time be one part of the absolute space into which the air passes; at another time it will be another part of the same, and so, absolutely understood, it will be continually changed.

III. Place is a part of space which a body takes up, and is according to the space, either absolute or relative. I say, a part of space; not the situation, nor the external surface of the body. For the places of equal solids are always equal; but their surfaces, by reason of their dissimilar figures, are often unequal. Positions properly have no quantity, nor are they so much the places themselves, as the properties of places. The motion of the whole is the same with the sum of the motions of the parts; that is, the translation of the whole, out of its place, is the same thing with the sum of the translations of the parts out of their places; and therefore the place of the whole is the same as the sum of the places of the parts, and for that reason, it is internal, and in the whole body.

IV. Absolute motion is the translation of a body from one absolute place into another; and relative motion, the translation from one relative place into another. Thus in a ship under sail, the relative place of a body is that part of the ship which the body possesses; or that part of the cavity which the body fills, and which therefore moves together with the ship: and relative rest is the continuance of the body in the same part of the ship, or of its cavity. But real, absolute rest, is the continuance of the body in the same part of that immovable space, in which the ship itself, its cavity, and all that it contains, is moved. Wherefore, if the earth is really at rest, the body, which relatively rests in the ship, will really and absolutely move with the same velocity which the ship has on the earth. But if the earth also moves, the true and absolute motion of the body will arise, partly from the true motion of the earth, in immovable space, partly from the relative motion of the ship on the earth; and if the body moves also relatively in the ship, its true motion will arise, partly from the true motion of the earth, in immovable space, and partly from the relative motions as well of the ship on the earth, as of the body in the ship; and from these relative motions will arise the relative motion of the body on the earth. As if that part of the earth, where the ship is, was truly moved towards the east, with a velocity of 10010 parts; while the ship itself, with a fresh gale, and full sails, is carried towards the west, with a velocity expressed by 10 of those parts; but a sailor walks in the ship towards the east, with 1 part of the said velocity; then the sailor will be moved truly in immovable space towards the east, with a velocity of 10001 parts, and relatively on the earth towards the west, with a velocity of 9 of those parts.

Absolute time, in astronomy, is distinguished from relative, by the equation or correction of the apparent time. For the natural days are truly unequal, though they are commonly considered as equal, and used for a measure of time; astronomers correct this inequality that they may measure the celestial motions by a more accurate time. It may be, that there is no such thing as an equable motion, whereby time may be accurately measured. All motions may be accelerated and retarded, but the flowing of absolute time is not liable to any change. The duration or perseverance of the existence of things remains the same, whether the motions are swift or slow, or none at all: and therefore this duration ought to be distinguished from what are only sensible measures thereof; and from which we deduce it, by means of the astronomical equation. The necessity of this equation, for determining the times of a phenomenon, is evinced as well from the experiments of the pendulum clock, as by eclipses of the satellites of Jupiter.

As the order of the parts of time is immutable, so also is the order of the parts of space. Suppose those parts to be moved out of their places, and they will be moved (if the expression may be allowed) out of themselves. For times and spaces are, as it were, the places as well of themselves as of all other things. All things are placed in time as to order of succession; and in space as to order of situation. It is from their essence or nature that they are places; and that the primary places of things should be movable, is absurd. These are therefore the absolute places; and translations out of those places, are the only absolute motions.

But because the parts of space cannot be seen, or distinguished from one another by our senses, therefore in their stead we use sensible measures of them. For from the positions and distances of things from any body considered as immovable, we define all places; and then with respect to such places, we estimate all motions, considering bodies as transferred from some of those places into others. And so, instead of absolute places and motions, we use relative ones; and that without any inconvenience in common affairs; but in philosophical disquisitions, we ought to abstract from our senses, and consider things themselves, distinct from what are only sensible measures of them. For it may be that there is no body really at rest, to which the places and motions of others may be referred.

But we may distinguish rest and motion, absolute and relative, one from the other by their properties, causes, and effects. It is a property of rest, that bodies really at rest do rest in respect to one another. And therefore as it is possible, that in the remote regions of the fixed stars, or perhaps far beyond them, there may be some body absolutely at rest; but impossible to know, from the position of bodies to one another in our regions, whether any of these do keep the same position to that remote body, it follows that absolute rest cannot be determined from the position of bodies in our regions.

It is a property of motion, that the parts, which retain given positions to their wholes, do partake of the motions of those wholes. For all the parts of revolving bodies endeavor to recede from the axis of motion; and the impetus of bodies moving forwards arises from the joint impetus of all the parts. Therefore, if surrounding bodies are moved, those that are relatively at rest within them will partake of their motion. Upon which account, the true and absolute motion of a body cannot be determined by the translation of it from those which only seem to rest; for the external bodies ought not only to appear at rest, but to be really at rest. For otherwise, all included bodies, besides their translation from near the surrounding ones, partake likewise of their true motions; and though that translation were not made, they would not be really at rest, but only seem to be so. For the surrounding bodies stand in the like relation to the surrounded as the exterior part of a whole does to the interior, or as the shell does to the kernel; but if the shell moves, the kernel will also move, as being part of the whole, without any removal from near the shell.

A property, near akin to the preceding, is this, that if a place is moved, whatever is placed therein moves along with it; and therefore a body, which is moved from a place in motion, partakes also of the motion of its place. Upon which account, all motions, from places in motion, are no other than parts of entire and absolute motions; and every entire motion is composed of the motion of the body out of its first place, and the motion of this place out of its place; and so on, until we come to some immovable place, as in the before-mentioned example of the sailor. Wherefore, entire and absolute motions can be no otherwise determined than by immovable places; and for that reason I did before refer those absolute motions to immovable places, but relative ones to movable places. Now no other places are immovable but those that, from infinity to infinity, do all retain the same given position one to another; and upon this account must ever remain unmoved; and do thereby constitute immovable space.

The causes by which true and relative motions are distinguished, one from the other, are the forces impressed upon bodies to generate motion. True motion is neither generated nor altered, but by some force impressed upon the body moved; but relative motion may be generated or altered without any force impressed upon the body. For it is sufficient only to impress some force on other bodies with which the former is compared, that by their giving way, that relation may be changed, in which the relative rest or motion of this other body did consist. Again, true motion suffers always some change from any force impressed upon the moving body; but relative motion does not necessarily undergo any change by such forces. For if the same forces are likewise impressed on those other bodies, with which the comparison is made, that the relative position may be preserved, then that condition will be preserved in which the relative motion consists. And therefore any relative motion may be changed when the true motion remains unaltered, and the relative may be preserved when the true suffers some change. Thus, true motion by no means consists in such relations.

The effects which distinguish absolute from relative motion are, the forces of receding from the axis of circular motion. For there are no such forces in a circular motion purely relative, but in a true and absolute circular motion, they are greater or less, according to the quantity of the motion. If a vessel, hung by a long cord, is so often turned about that the cord is strongly twisted, then filled with water, and held at rest together with the water; thereupon, by the sudden action of another force, it is whirled about the contrary way, and while the cord is untwisting itself, the vessel continues for some time in this motion; the surface of the water will at first be plain, as before the vessel began to move; but after that, the vessel, by gradually communicating its motion to the water, will make it begin sensibly to revolve, and recede by little and little from the middle, and ascend to the sides of the vessel, forming itself into a concave figure (as I have experienced), and the swifter the motion becomes, the higher will the water rise, till at last, performing its revolutions in the same times with the vessel, it becomes relatively at rest in it. This ascent of the water shows its endeavor to recede from the axis of its motion; and the true and absolute circular motion of the water, which is here directly contrary to the relative, becomes known, and may be measured by this endeavor. At first, when the relative motion of the water in the vessel was greatest, it produced no endeavor to recede from the axis; the water showed no tendency to the circumference, nor any ascent towards the sides of the vessel, but remained of a plain surface, and therefore its true circular motion had not yet begun. But afterwards, when the relative motion of the water had decreased, the ascent thereof towards the sides of the vessel proved its endeavor to recede from the axis; and this endeavor showed the real circular motion of the water continually increasing, till it had acquired its greatest quantity, when the water rested relatively in the vessel. And therefore this endeavor does not depend upon any translation of the water in respect of the ambient bodies, nor can true circular motion be defined by such translation. There is only one real circular motion of any one revolving body, corresponding to only one power of endeavoring to recede from its axis of motion, as its proper and adequate effect; but relative motions, in one and the same body, are innumerable, according to the various relations it bears to external bodies, and, like other relations, are altogether destitute of any real effect, any otherwise than they may perhaps partake of that one only true motion. And therefore in their system who suppose that our heavens, revolving below the sphere of the fixed stars, carry the planets along with them; the several parts of those heavens, and the planets, which are indeed relatively at rest in their heavens, do yet really move. For they change their position one to another (which never happens to bodies truly at rest), and being carried together with their heavens, partake of their motions, and as parts of revolving wholes, endeavor to recede from the axis of their motions.

Wherefore relative quantites are not the quantities themselves, whose names they bear, but those sensible measures of them (either accurate or inaccurate), which are commonly used instead of the measured quantites themselves. And if the meaning of words is to be determined by their use, then by the names time, space, place, and motion, their [sensible] measures are properly to be understood; and the expression will be unusual, and purely mathematical, if the measured quantities themselves are meant. On this account, those violate the accuracy of language, which ought to be kept precise, who interpret these words for the measured quantities. Nor do those less defile the purity of mathematical and philosophical truths, who confound real quantities with their relations and sensible measures.

It is indeed a matter of great difficulty to discover, and effectually to distinguish, the true motions of particular bodies from the apparent; because the parts of that immovable space, in which those motions are performed, do by no means come under the observation of our senses. Yet the thing is not altogether desperate; for we have some arguments to guide us, partly from the apparent motions, which are the differences of the true motions; partly from the forces, which are the causes and effects of the true motions. For instance, if two globes, kept at a given distance one from the other by means of a cord that connects them, were revolved about their common centre of gravity, we might, from the tension of the cord, discover the endeavor of the globes to recede from the axis of their motion, and from thence we might compute the quantity of their circular motions. And then if any equal forces should be impressed at once on the alternate faces of the globes to augment or diminish their circular motions, from the increase or decrease of the tenison of the cord, we might infer the increment or decrement of their motions; and thence would be found on what faces those forces ought to be impressed, that the motions of the globes might be most augmented; that is, we might discover their hindmost faces, or those which, in the circular motion, do follow. But the faces which follow being known, and consequently the opposite ones that precede, we should likewise know the determination of their motions. And thus we might find both the quantity and the determination of this circular motion, even in an immense vacuum, where there was nothing external or sensible with which the globes could be compared. But now, if in that space some remote bodies were placed that kept always a given position one to another, as the fixed stars do in our regions, we could not indeed determine from the relative translation of the globes among those bodies, whether the motion did belong to the globes or to the bodies. But if we observed the cord, and found that its tension was that very tension which the motions of the globes required, we might conclude the motion to be in the globes, and the bodies to be at rest; and then, lastly, from the translation of the globes among the bodies, we should find the determination of their motions. But how we are to obtain the true motions from their causes, effects, and apparent differences, and the converse, shall be explained more at large in the following treatise. For to this end it was that I composed it.

RULES OF REASONING IN PHILOSOPHY

Rule I

We are to admit no more causes of natural things than such as are both true and sufficient to explain their appearances. To this purpose the philosophers say that Nature does nothing in vain, and more is in vain when less will serve; for Nature is pleased with simplicity, and affects not the pomp of superfluous causes.

Rule II

Therefore to the same natural effects we must, as far as possible, assign the same causes. As to respiration in a man and in a beast; the descent of stones in *Europe* and in *America*; the light of our culinary fire and of the sun; the reflection of light in the earth, and in the planets.

Rule III

The qualities of bodies, which admit neither intensification nor remission of degrees, and which are found to belong to all bodies within the reach of our experiments, are to be esteemed the universal qualities of all bodies whatsoever. For since the qualities of bodies are only known to us by experiments, we are to hold for universal all such as universally agree with experiments; and such as are not liable to diminution can never be quite taken away. We are certainly not to relinquish the evidence of experiments for the sake of dreams and vain fictions of our own devising; nor are we to recede from the analogy of Nature, which is wont to be simple, and always consonant to itself. We no other way know the extension of bodies than by our senses, nor do these reach it in all bodies; but because we perceive extension in all that are sensible, therefore we ascribe it universally to all others also. That abundance of bodies are hard, we learn by experience; and because the hardness of the whole arises from the hardness of the parts, we therefore justly infer the hardness of the undivided particles not only of the bodies we feel but of all others. That all bodies are impenetrable, we gather not from reason, but from sensation. The bodies which we handle we find impenetrable, and thence conclude impenetrability to be an universal property of all bodies whatsoever. That all bodies are movable, and endowed with certain powers (which we call the inertia) of persevering in their motion, or in their rest, we only infer from the like properties observed in the bodies which we have seen. The extension, hardness, impenetrability, mobility, and inertia of the whole, result from the extension, hardness, impenetrability, mobility, and inertia of the parts; and hence we conclude the least particles of all bodies to be also all extended, and hard and impenetrable, and movable, and endowed with their proper inertia. And this is the foundation of all philosophy. Moreover, that the divided but contiguous particles of bodies may be separated from one another, is matter of observation; and, in the particles that remain undivided, our minds are able to distinguish yet lesser parts, as is mathematically demonstrated. But whether the parts so distinguished, and not yet divided, may, by the powers of Nature, be actually divided and separated from ane another, we cannot certainly determine. Yet, had we the proof of but one experiment that any undivided particle, in breaking a hard and solid body, suffered a division, we might by virtue of this rule conclude that the undivided as well as the divided particles may be divided and actually separated to infinity.

Lastly, if it universally appears, by experiments and astronomical observations, that all bodies about the earth gravitate towards the earth, and that in proportion to the quantity of matter which they severally contain; that the moon likewise, according to the quantity of its matter, gravitates towards the earth; that, on the other hand, our sea gravitates towards the moon; and all the planets one towards another; and the comets in like manner towards the sun; we must, in consequence of this rule, universally allow that all bodies whatsoever are endowed with a principle of mutual gravitation. For the argument from the appearances concludes with more force for the universal gravitation of all bodies than for their impenetrability; of which, among those in the celestial regions, we have no experiments, nor any manner of observation. Not that I affirm gravity to be essential to bodies: by their *vis insita* I mean nothing but their inertia. This is immutable. Their gravity is diminished as they recede from the earth.

Rule IV

In experimental philosophy we are to look upon propositions inferred by general induction from phenomena as accurately or very nearly true, notwithstanding any contrary hypotheses that may be imagined, till such time as other phenomena occur, by which they may either be made more accurate, or liable to exceptions. This rule we must follow, that the argument of induction may not be evaded by hypotheses.

GENERAL SCHOLIUM

The hypothesis of vortices is pressed with many difficulties. That every planet by a radius drawn to the sun may describe areas proportional to the times of description, the periodic times of the several parts of the vortices should observe the square of their distances from the sun; but that the periodic times of the planets may obtain the ³⁄₂th power of their distances from the sun, the periodic times of the parts of the vortex ought to be as the ³⁄₂th power of their distances. That the smaller vortices may maintain their lesser revolutions about Saturn, Jupiter, and other planets, and swim quietly and undisturbed in the greater vortex of the sun, the periodic times of the parts of the sun's vortex should be equal; but the rotation of the sun and planets about their axes, which ought to correspond with the motions of their vortices, recede far from all these proportions. The motions of the comets are exceedingly regular, are governed by the same laws with the motions of the planets, and can by no means be accounted for by the hypothesis of vortices; for comets are carried with very eccentric motions through all parts of the heavens indifferently, with a freedom that is incompatible with the notion of a vortex.

Bodies projected in our air suffer no resistance but from the air.

Withdraw the air, as is done in Mr. *Boyle's* vacuum, and the resistance ceases; for in this void a bit of fine down and a piece of solid gold descend with equal velocity. And the same argument must apply to the celestial spaces above the earth's atmosphere; in these spaces, where there is no air to resist their motions, all bodies will move with the greatest freedom; and the planets and comets will constantly pursue their revolutions in orbits given in kind and position, according to the laws above explained; but though these bodies may, indeed, continue in their orbits by the mere laws of gravity, yet they could by no means have at first derived the regular position of the orbits themselves from those laws.

The six primary planets are revolved about the sun in circles concentric with the sun, and with motions directed towards the same parts, and almost in the same plane. Ten moons are revolved about the earth, Jupiter, and Saturn, in circles concentric with them, with the same direction of motion, and nearly in the planes of the orbits of those planets; but it is not to be conceived that mere mechanical causes could give birth to so many regular motions, since the comets range over all parts of the heavens in very eccentric orbits; for by that kind of motion they pass easily through the orbs of the planets, and with great rapidity; and in their aphelions, where they move the slowest, and are detained the longest, they recede to the greatest distances from each other, and hence suffer the least disturbance from their mutual attractions. This most beautiful system of the sun, planets, and comets, could only proceed from the counsel and dominion of an intelligent and powerful Being. And if the fixed stars are the centres of other like systems, these, being formed by the like wise counsel, must be all subject to the dominion of One; especially since the light of the fixed stars is of the same nature with the light of the sun, and from every system light passes into all the other systems; and lest the systems of the fixed stars should, by their gravity, fall on each other, he hath placed those systems at immense distances from one another.

This Being governs all things, not as the soul of the world, but

---

1. Dr. *Pocock* derives the Latin word *Deus* from the *Arabic du* (in the oblique case *di*), which signifies *Lord*. And in this sense princes are called *gods, Psal.* lxxxii. ver. 6; and *John* x. ver. 35. And *Moses* is called a *god* to his brother *Aaron*, and a *god* to *Pharaoh* (*Exod.* iv. ver. 16; and vii. ver. 1). And in the same sense the souls of dead princes were formerly, by the Heathens, called *gods*, but falsely, because of their want of dominion.

as Lord over all; and on account of his dominion he is wont to be called *Lord God* παντσκράτωρ, or *Universal Ruler*; for *God* is a relative word, and has a respect to servants; and *Deity* in the dominion of God not over his own body, as those imagine who fancy God to be the soul of the world, but over servants. The Supreme God is a Being eternal, infinite, absolutely perfect; but a being, however perfect, without dominion, cannot be said to be Lord God; for we say, my God, your God, the God of *Israel*, the God of Gods, and Lord of Lords; but we do not say, my Eternal, your Eternal, the Eternal of *Israel*, the Eternal of Gods; we do not say, my Infinite, or my Perfect: these are titles which have no respect to servants. The word God[1] usually signifies *Lord*; but every lord is not a God. It is the dominion of a spiritual being which constitutes a God: a true, supreme, or imaginary dominion makes a true, supreme, or imaginary God. And from his true dominion it follows that the true God is a living, intelligent, and powerful Being; and from his other perfections, that he is supreme, or most perfect. He is eternal and infinite, omnipotent and omniscient; that is, his duration reaches from eternity to eternity; his presence from infinity to infinity; he governs all things, and knows all things that are or can be done. He is not eternity and infinity, but eternal and infinite; he is not duration or space, but he endures and is present. He endures forever, and is everywhere present; and, by existing always and everywhere, he constitutes duration and space. Since every particle of space is *always*, and every indivisible moment of duration is *everywhere*, certainly the Maker and Lord of all things cannot be *never* and *nowhere*. Every soul that has perception is, though in different times and in different organs of sense and motion, still the same indivisible person. There are given successive parts in duration, coexistent parts in space, but neither the one nor the other in the person of a man, or his thinking principle; and much less can they be found in the thinking substance of God. Every man, so far as he is a thing that has perception, is one and the same man during his whole life, in all and each of his organs of sense. God is the same God, always and everywhere. He is omnipresent not *virtually* only, but also *substantially*; for virtue cannot subsist without substance. In him[2] are all things contained and moved; yet neither

---

2. This was the opinion of the Ancients. So *Pythagoras*, in *Cicer. de Nat. Deor.* lib. i. *Thales, Anaxagoras, Virgil*, Georg. lib. iv. ver. 220; and Aeneid, lib. vi. ver. 721. *Philo*

affects the other: God suffers nothing from the motion of bodies; bodies find no resistance from the omnipresence of God. It is allowed by all that the Supreme God exists necessarily; and by the same necessity he exists *always* and *everywhere*. Whence also he is all similar, all eye, all ear, all brain, all arm, all power to perceive, to understand, and to act; but in a manner not at all human, in a manner not at all corporeal, in a manner utterly unknown to us. As a blind man has no idea of colors, so have we no idea of the manner by which the all-wise God perceives and understands all things. He is utterly void of all body and bodily figure, and can therefore neither be seen, nor heard, nor touched; nor ought he to be worshiped under the representation of any corporeal thing. We have ideas of his attributes, but what the real substance of anything is we know not. In bodies, we see only their figures and colors, we hear only the sounds, we touch only their outward surfaces, we smell only the smells, and taste the savors; but their inward substances are not to be known either by our senses, or by any reflex act of our minds: much less, then, have we any idea of the substance of God. We know him only by his most wise and excellent contrivances of things, and final causes; we admire him for his perfections; but we reverence and adore him on account of his dominion: for we adore him as his servants; and a god without dominion, providence, and final causes, is nothing else but Fate and Nature. Blind metaphysical necessity, which is certainly the same always and everywhere, could produce no variety of things. All that diversity of natural things which we find suited to different times and places could arise from nothing but the ideas and will of a Being necessarily existing. But, by way of allegory, God is said to see, to speak, to laugh, to love, to hate, to desire, to give, to receive, to rejoice, to be angry, to fight, to frame, to work, to build; for all our notions of God are taken from the ways of mankind by a certain similitude, which, though not perfect, has some likeness, however. And thus much concerning God; to discourse of whom

---

Allegor, at the beginning of lib. i. *Aratus,* in his Phaenom. at the beginning. So also the sacred writers: as St. *Paul, Acts* xvii. ver. 27, 28. St. *John's* Gosp. chap. xiv. ver. 2. *Moses,* in *Deut.* iv. ver. 39; and x. ver. 14. *David, Psal.* cxxxix, ver. 7, 8, 9. *Solomon,* 1 *Kings* viii ver. 27. *Job,* xxii. ver. 12, 13, 14. *Jeremiah,* xxiii. ver. 23, 24. The Idolaters supposed the sun, moon, and stars, the souls of men, and other parts of the world, to be parts of the Supreme God, and therefore to be worshiped; but erroneously.

from the appearances of things, does certainly belong to Natural Philosophy.

Hitherto we have explained the phenomena of the heavens and of our sea by the power of gravity, but have not yet assigned the cause of this power. This is certain, that it must proceed from a cause that penetrates to the very centres of the sun and planets, without suffering the least diminution of its force; that operates not according to the quantity of the surfaces of the particles upon which it acts (as mechanical causes used to do), but according to the quantity of the solid matter which they contain, and propagates its virtue on all sides to immense distances, decreasing always as the inverse square of the distances. Gravitation towards the sun is made up out of the gravitations towards the several particles of which the body of the sun is composed; and in receding from the sun decreases accurately as the inverse square of the distances as far as the orbit of Saturn, as evidently appears from the quiescence of the aphelion of the planets; nay, and even to the remotest aphelion of the comets, if those aphelions are also quiescent. But hitherto I have not been able to discover the cause of those properties of gravity from phenomena, and I frame no hypotheses; for whatever is not deduced from the phenomena is to be called an hypothesis; and hypotheses, whether metaphysical or physical, whether of occult qualities or mechanical, have no place in experimental philosophy. In this philosophy particular propositions are inferred from the phenomena, and afterwards rendered general by induction. Thus it was that the impenetrability, the mobility, and the impulsive force of bodies, and the laws of motion and of gravitation, were discovered. And to us it is enough that gravity does really exist, and act according to the laws which we have explained, and abundantly serves to account for all the motions of the celestial bodies, and of our sea.

And now we might add something concerning a certain most subtle spirit which pervades and lies hid in all gross bodies; by the force and action of which spirit the particles of bodies attract one another at near distances, and cohere, if contiguous; and electric bodies operate to greater distances, as well repelling as attracting the neighboring corpuscles; and light is emitted, reflected, refracted, inflected, and heats bodies; and all sensation is excited, and the members of animal bodies move at the command of the will, namely, by the vibrations of this spirit, mutually propagated along the solid filaments of the nerves, from the outward organs of sense to the brain, and from the brain into the muscles. But these are things that cannot be explained in few words, nor are we furnished with that sufficiency of experiments which is required to an accurate determination and demonstration of the laws by which this electric and elastic spirit operates.

OPTICKS

QUERY 31

And thus Nature will be very conformable to her self and very simple, performing all the great Motions of the heavenly Bodies by the Attraction of Gravity which intercedes those Bodies, and almost all the small ones of their Particles by some other attractive and repelling Powers which intercede the Particles. The *Vis inertiæ* is a passive Principle by which Bodies persist in their Motion or Rest, receive Motion in proportion to the Force impressing it, and resist as much as they are resisted. By this Principle alone there never could have been any Motion in the World. Some other Principle was necessary for putting Bodies into Motion; and now they are in Motion, some other Principle is necessary for conserving the Motion. For from the various Composition of two Motions, 'tis very certain that there is not always the same quantity of Motion in the World. For if two Globes joined by a slender Rod, revolve about their common Center of Gravity with an uniform Motion, while that Center moves on uniformly in a right Line drawn in the Plane of their circular Motion; the Sum of the Motions of the two Globes, as often as the Globes are in the right Line described by their common Center of Gravity, will be bigger than the Sum of their Motions, when they are in a Line perpendicular to that right Line. By this Instance it appears that Motion may be got or lost. But by reason of the Tenacity of Fluids, and Attrition of their Parts, and the Weakness of Elasticity in Solids, Motion is much more apt to be lost than got, and is always upon the Decay. For Bodies which are either absolutely hard, or so soft as to be void of Elasticity, will not rebound from one another. Impenetrability makes them only stop. If two equal Bodies meet directly *in vacuo*, they will by the Laws of Motion stop where they meet, and lose all their Motion, and remain in rest, unless they be elastick, and receive new Motion from their Spring. If they have so much Elasticity as suffices to make them re-bound with a quarter, or half, or three quarters of the Force with which they come together, they will lose three quarters, or half, or a quarter of their Motion. And this may be try'd, by letting two equal Pendulums fall against one another from equal heights. If the Pendulums be of Lead or soft Clay, they will lose all or almost all their Motions: If of elastick Bodies they will lose all but what they recover from their Elasticity. If it be said, that they can lose no Motion but what they communicate to other Bodies, the consequence is, that *in vacuo* they can lose no Motion, but when they meet they must go on and penetrate one another's Dimensions. If three equal round Vessels be filled, the one with Water, the other with Oil, the third with molten Pitch, and the Liquors be stirred about alike to give them a vortical Motion; the Pitch by its Tenacity will lose its Motion quickly, the Oil being less tenacious will keep it longer, and the Water being less tenacious will keep it longest, but yet will lose it in a short time. Whence it is easy to understand, that if many contiguous Vortices of molten Pitch were each of them as large as those which some suppose to revolve about the Sun and fix'd Stars, yet these and all their Parts would, by their Tenacity and Stiffness, communicate their Motion to one another till they all rested among themselves. Vortices of Oil or Water, or some fluider Matter, might continue longer in Motion; but unless the Matter were void of all Tenacity and Attrition of Parts, and Communication of Motion, (which is not to be supposed,) the Motion would constantly decay. Seeing therefore the variety of Motion which we find in the World is always decreasing, there is a necessity of conserving and recruiting it by active Principles, such as are the cause of Gravity, by which Planets and Comets keep their Motions in their Orbs, and Bodies acquire great Motion in falling; and the cause of Fermentation, by which the Heart and Blood of Animals are kept in perpetual Motion and Heat; the inward Parts of the Earth are constantly warm'd, and in some places grow very hot; Bodies burn and shine, Mountains take fire, the Caverns of the Earth are blown up, and the Sun continues violently hot and lucid, and warms all things by his Light. For we meet with very little Motion in the World, besides what is owing to these active Principles. And if it were not for these Principles, the Bodies of the Earth, Planets, Comets, Sun, and all things in them, would grow cold and freeze, and become inactive Masses; and all Putrefaction, Generation, Vegetation and Life would cease, and the Planets and Comets would not remain in their Orbs.

All these things being consider'd, it seems probable to me, that God in the Beginning form'd Matter in solid, massy, hard, impenetrable, moveable Particles, of such Sizes and Figures, and with such other Properties, and in such Proportion to Space, as most conduced to the End for which he form'd them; and that these primitive Particles being Solids, are incomparably harder than any porous Bodies compounded of them; even so very hard, as never to wear or break in pieces; no ordinary Power being able to divide what God himself made one in the first Creation. While the Particles continue entire, they may compose Bodies of one and the same Nature and Texture in all Ages: But should they wear away, or break in pieces, the Nature of Things depending on them, would be changed. Water and Earth, composed of old worn Particles and Fragments of Particles, would not be of the same Nature and Texture now, with Water and Earth composed of entire Particles in the Beginning. And therefore, that Nature may be lasting, the Changes of corporeal Things are to be placed only in the various Separations and new Associations and Motions of these permanent Particles; compound Bodies being apt to break, not in the midst of solid Particles, but where those Particles are laid together, and only touch in a few Points.

It seems to me farther, that these Particles have not only a *Vis inertiæ*, accompanied with such passive Laws of Motion as naturally result from that Force, but also that they are moved by certain active Principles, such as is that of Gravity, and that which causes Fermentation, and the Cohesion of Bodies. These Principles I consider, not as occult Qualities, supposed to result from the specifick Forms of Things, but as general Laws of Nature, by which the Things themselves are form'd; their Truth appearing to us by Phaenomena, though their Causes be not yet discover'd. For these are manifest Qualities, and their Causes only are occult. And the *Aristotelians* gave the Name of occult Qualities, not to manifest Qualities, but to such Qualities only as they supposed to lie hid in Bodies, and to be the unknown Causes of manifest Effects: Such as would be the Causes of Gravity, and of magnetick and electrick Attractions, and of Fermentations, if we should suppose that these Forces or Actions arose from Qualities unknown to us, and uncapable of being discovered and made manifest. Such occult Qualities put a stop to the Improvement of natural Philosophy, and therefore of late Years have been rejected. To tell us that every Species of Things is endow'd with an occult specifick Quality by which it acts and produces manifest Effects, is to tell us nothing: But to derive two or three general Principles of Motion from Phaenomena, and afterwards to tell us how the Properties and Actions of all corporeal Things follow from those manifest Principles, would be a very great step in Philosophy, though the Causes of those Principles were not yet discover'd: And therefore I scruple not to propose the Principles of Motion above-mention'd, they being of very general Extent, and leave their Causes to be found out.

Now by the help of these Principles, all material Things seem to have been composed of the hard and solid Particles above-mention'd, variously associated in the first Creation by the Counsel of an intelligent Agent. For it became him who created them to set them in order. And if he did so, it's unphilosophical to seek for any other Origin of the World, or to pretend that it might arise out of a Chaos by the mere Laws of Nature; though being once form'd, it may continue by those Laws for many Ages. For while Comets move in very excentrick Orbs in all manner of Positions, blind Fate could never make all the Planets move one and the same way in Orbs concentrick, some inconsiderable Irregularities excepted, which may have risen from the mutual Actions of Comets and Planets upon one another, and which will be apt to increase, till this System wants a Reformation. Such a wonderful Uniformity in the Planetary System must be allowed the Effect of Choice. And so must the Uniformity in the Bodies of Animals, they having generally a right and a left side shaped alike, and on either side of their Bodies two Legs behind, and either two Arms, or two Legs, or two Wings before upon their Shoulders, and between their Shoulders a Neck running down into a Back-bone, and a Head upon it; and in the Head two Ears, two Eyes, a Nose, a Mouth, and a Tongue, alike situated. Also the first Contrivance of those very artificial Parts of Animals, the Eyes, Ears, Brain, Muscles, Heart, Lungs, Midriff, Glands, Larynx, Hands, Wings, swimming Bladders, natural Spectacles, and other Organs of Sense and Motion; and the Instinct of Brutes and Insects, can be the effect of nothing else than the Wisdom and Skill of a powerful ever-living Agent, who being in all Places, is more able by his Will to move the Bodies within his boundless uniform Sensorium, and thereby to form and reform the Parts of the Universe, than we are by our Will to move the Parts of our own Bodies. And yet we are not to consider the World as the Body of God, or the several Parts thereof, as the Parts of God. He is an uniform Being, void of Organs, Members or Parts, and they are his Creatures subordinate to him, and subservient to his Will; and he is no more the Soul of them, than the Soul of Man is the Soul of the Species of Things carried through the Organs of Sense into the place of its Sensation, where it perceives them by means of its immediate Presence, without the Intervention of any third thing. The Organs of Sense are not for enabling the Soul to perceive the Species of Things in its Sensorium, but only for conveying them thither; and God has no need of such Organs, he being every where present to the Things themselves. And since Space is divisible *in infinitum*, and Matter is not necessarily in all places, it may be also allow'd that God is able to create Particles of Matter of several Sizes and Figures, and in several Proportions to Space, and perhaps of different Densities and Forces, and thereby to vary the Laws of Nature, and make Worlds of several sorts in several Parts of the Universe. At least, I see nothing of Contradiction in all this.

As in Mathematicks, so in Natural Philosophy, the Investigation of difficult Things by the Method of Analysis, ought ever to precede the Method of Composition. This Analysis consists in making Experiments and Observations, and in drawing general Conclusions from them by Induction, and admitting of no Objections against the Conclusions, but such as are taken from Experiments, or other certain Truths. For Hypotheses are not to be regarded in experimental Philosophy. And although the arguing from Experiments and Observations by Induction be no Demonstration of general Conclusions; yet it is the best way of arguing which the Nature of Things admits of, and may be looked upon as so much the stronger, by how much the Induction is more general. And if no Exception occur from Phænomena, the Conclusion may be pronounced generally. But if at any time afterwards any Exception shall occur from Experiments, it may then begin to be pronounced with such Exceptions as occur. By this way of Analysis we may proceed from Compounds to Ingredients, and from Motions to the Forces producing them; and in general, from Effects to their Causes, and from particular Causes to more general ones, till the Argument ends in the most general. This is the Method of Analysis: And the Synthesis consists in assuming the Causes discover'd, and establish'd as Principles, and by them explaining the Phaenomena proceeding from them, and proving the Explanations.

In the two first Books of these Opticks, I proceeded by this Analysis to discover and prove the original Differences of the Rays of Light in respect of Refrangibility, Reflexibility, and Colour, and their alternate Fits of easy Reflexion and easy Transmision, and the Properties of Bodies, both opake and pellucid, on which their Reflexions and Colours depend. And these Discoveries being proved, may be assumed in the Method of Composition for explaining the Phaenomena arising from them: An Instance of which Method I gave in the End of the first Book. In this third Book I have only begun the Analysis of what remains to be discover'd about Light and its Effects upon the Frame of Nature, hinting several things about it, and leaving the Hints to be examin'd and improv'd by the farther Experiments and Observations of such as are inquisitive. And if natural Philosophy in all its parts, by pursuing this Method, shall at length be perfected, the Bounds of Moral Philosophy will be also enlarged. For so far as we can know by natural Philosophy what is the first Cause, what Power he has over us, and what Benefits we receive from him, so far our Duty towards him, as well as that towards one another, will appear to us by the Light of Nature. And no doubt, if the Worship of false Gods had not blinded the Heathen, their moral Philosophy would have gone farther than to the four Cardinal Virtues; and instead of teaching the Transmigration of Souls, and to worship the Sun and Moon, and dead Heroes, they would have taught us to worship our true Author and Benefactor, as their Ancestors did under the Government of *Noah* and his Sons before they corrupted themselves.

CHRONOLOGY

Columbus in America	**1492**	
Nicolaus Copernicus	(1473–1543)	*De Revolutionibus,* 1543
Luther's 95 Theses	**1517**	
William Gilbert	(1544–1603)	*On the Magnet,* 1600
Spanish Armada defeated	**1588**	
Tycho Brahe	(1564–1601)	
Francis Bacon	(1561–1626)	*The New Organon,* 1620
William Shakespeare	(1564–1616)	
Galileo Galilei	(1564–1642)	*The Starry Messenger,* 1610
		Two Chief World Systems, 1633
		Two New Sciences, 1638
Johannes Kepler	(1571–1630)	*Harmonices Mundi,* 1619
John Donne	(1572–1631)	
William Harvey	(1578–1657)	*The Circulation of Blood,* 1628
Harvard College founded	**1636**	
Thomas Hobbes	(1588–1679)	*Leviathan,* 1651
Pierre Gassendi	(1592–1655)	*Disquisitio Metaphysica,* 1644
René Descartes	(1596–1650)	*Principles of Philosophy,* 1644
English Civil War	**1642–1646**	
Rembrandt van Rijn	(1606–1669)	
John Milton	(1608–1674)	
Blaise Pascal	(1623–1662)	

Robert Boyle	(1627–1691)	*Skeptical Chymist,* 1661
Christian Huygens	(1629–1695)	*Treatise on Light,* 1690
John Locke	(1632–1704)	*Essay Concerning Human Under-standing,* 1690
Benedict de Spinoza	(1632–1677)	*Ethics,* 1678
Robert Hooke	(1635–1703)	*Micrographia,* 1665
Isaac Newton	(1642–1727)	*Principia,* 1687 *Opticks,* 1704
Gottfried W. von Leibniz	(1646–1716)	*New System of Nature,* 1695
George Berkeley	(1685–1753)	*Principles of Human Knowledge,* 1710
Benjamin Franklin	(1706–1790)	*Experiments and Observations on Electricity,* 1751
David Hume	(1711–1776)	*Enquiry Concerning Human Under-standing,* 1751
American Revolution	**1776**	
Immanuel Kant	(1724–1804)	*Critique of Pure Reason,* 1781

Bibliography

Amsterdamski, Stefan. *Between Experience & Metaphysics: Philosophical Problems of the Evolution of Science.* Boston: Reidel, 1975.

Blumenberg, Hans. *The Genesis of the Copernican World.* Cambridge, Mass.: MIT Press, 1987.

Boas, Marie. *The Scientific Renaissance 1450–1630.* New York: Harper & Row, 1962.

Buchdahl, Gerd. *Metaphysics & the Philosophy of Science.* Oxford: Basil Blackwell, 1969.

Burtt, E.A. *The Metaphysical Foundations of Modern Physical Science.* London: Routledge & Kegan Paul, 1924.

Clagett, Marshall. *The Science of Mechanics in the Middle Ages.* Madison: University of Wisconsin Press, 1959.

Cohen, I. Bernard. *The Newtonian Revolution.* Cambridge: Cambridge University Press, 1980.

Dyksterhuis, E.J. *The Mechanization of the World Picture.* Princeton: Princeton University Press, 1986.

Duhem, Pierre. *To Save the Phenomena: An Essay on the Development of Physical Theory from Plato to Galileo.* Chicago: University of Chicago Press, 1969 (orig. 1908).

Freudenthal, Gideon. *Atom & Individual in the Age of Newton: On the Genesis of the Mechanistic World View.* Boston: Reidel, 1986.

Gillispie, Charles C. *The Edge of Objectivity: An Essay on the History of Scientific Ideas.* Princeton: Princeton University Press, 1960.

Hall, A.R. *The Scientific Revolution 1500–1800: The Formation of the Modern Scientific Attitude.* Boston: Beacon Press, 1954.

Harré, Rom. *Matter & Method.* London: Macmillan, 1964.

Holton, Gerald. *Thematic Origins of Scientific Thought: Kepler to Einstein.* Cambridge, Mass.: Harvard University Press, 1973.

Koyré, Alexandre. *From the Closed World to the Infinite Universe.* Baltimore: Johns Hopkins University Press, 1957.

Wartofsky, Marx. *Models: Representation & the Scientific Understanding.* Boston: Reidel, 1979.

Westfall, Richard S. *The Construction of Modern Science: Mechanism & Mechanics.* New York: John Wiley & Sons, 1971.

This book was set in
Baskerville
by
J. Jarrett Engineering, Inc.

Baskerville
is a modern typeface
developed from faces
originally designed by
the English typographer
John Baskerville
(1706–1775)